JUAN MARTÍN'S
Guitar Method

EL ARTE FLAMENCO
DE LA GUITARRA

ALSO AVAILABLE:

A 60-minute compact
disc or cassette recording
of music contained in
this volume, composed
and played

by

JUAN MARTÍN

 United Music Publishers Ltd
42 Rivington Street London EC2A 3BN

The secrets of Flamenco, that 'wonder of natural art' as Manuel de Falla called it, have hitherto been hard to learn without personal lessons from an expert teacher, and such teachers are rare indeed outside Andalucía or Madrid. Yet nearly everyone who plays or wants to play the Spanish guitar would like to learn at least something about how those exciting sounds of Flamenco are created. Here now is a book combined with a cassette tape-recording in which a top-ranking flamenco soloist and recording artist reveals the very essence of the flamenco art of the guitar.

Juan Martín's playing of his music on the cassette, along with the many photographs and details in the text, vividly demonstrates the essential techniques, rhythms and *toques* of Flamenco. His Method also contains longer solos, daily exercises for developing technique and invaluable information about the flamenco guitar and its music.

The Method has been designed for the player of any standard. You may be an absolute beginner with no previous knowledge of music or the guitar, or you may already play the guitar quite well. Your ambitions may be just to be able to enjoy yourself playing some Flamenco, or they may reach much further, perhaps even so far as pursuing a professional career with the guitar. Whatever the case, the Method will provide the basis for you to advance greatly your skill and understanding, so that you find in the joys and sorrows of Flamenco something more of that capacity for expressing oneself through the guitar which Juan Martín so excitingly demonstrates.

Juan Martín

Juan Martín is a celebrated virtuoso of the flamenco guitar who has been voted into the top three guitarists in the world by the US magazine 'Guitar Player'. He is a phenomenal player who has established an international name for himself as one of today's most exciting and most creative performers of Flamenco. In addition, he is an inspiring teacher with a passionate enthusiasm for communicating his enjoyment and knowledge of the art to others. Such generous commitment of energy to this labour of love is especially remarkable because flamenco guitarists tend by tradition to be very reticent, even secretive, about how they play.

Juan Martín's artistry has evolved in the very purest of traditions of Flamenco. From his early years in Malaga, one of the great historic centres of Flamenco, he went on to gain wide experience playing with many of Spain's leading singers and dancers before attaining his present eminence as a solo recitalist and recording star. In London he has given many recitals at the Barbican, Queen Elizabeth and Wigmore Halls and is often asked to play on television and radio. In Madrid he has played to a very large audience in the prestigious Palacio de Congresos and tours internationally with the Juan Martín Flamenco Dance Company. He has performed at major international arts festivals including Edinburgh, Ludwigsburg, Montreux, Istanbul and Hong Kong. Television appearances include CNN TV (worldwide), Radio Television Española, BBC UK and ZDF Germany. In Andalucia itself he has appeared in *Cante Flamenco* festivals and had the honour of being invited to play at Picasso's 90th birthday celebration. In 1992 he recorded the high definition television film for the EEC pavillion at the EXPO in Seville.

For a flamenco guitarist to achieve such distinction, he must have more than just brilliant technique which one hears on his solo CDs. In the art of Juan Martín one can quickly identify that extra-special magic as an uncompromising 'flamenconess' which comes from the soul. His compositions for the guitar show an exceptionally wide-ranging mastery of rhythm and expression and a profound respect of the oldest traditions and origins of Flamenco. A deep understanding of the flamenco *Cante*, a rare distillation of experience which inspires much of his music, is a special hallmark of his style, as was memorably demonstrated in a London concert with the legendary gypsy singer, Rafael Romero. Above all, his playing is powered by an earthy intensity of rhythm and emotion (or, to put it simply, *duende*) which is the true heart of Flamenco.

Introduction by Juan Martín

This is a book for those genuinely interested in learning the marvellous art of the flamenco guitar. I have tried to convey in my method the exact way traditional technique is built and the purest playing style achieved. The rhythms and melodic variations (falsetas) are the very basis upon which all good professional flamencos base their style. I have taken particular care to show in the music the correct fingering for both hands for this is often the problem for players learning by ear from recordings. (The book starts at the very beginning and assumes no knowledge of Flamenco or music on the part of the beginner). The music contained is also written in cifra which is explained at the start for those who do not know or wish to learn music. The transcription of the music, together with the preparation of the text and of the photos showing the way I play, has been undertaken by my good friend and guitarist Patrick Campbell; an exhausting task completed with great love.

The great and ancient tradition of Flamenco is a broad and deep current formed from many sources. I would like to dedicate this book not only to all those new aficionados I hope it will encourage but also to all those many unsung players of the flamenco guitar whose playing continually enriches and extends the tradition of Flamenco. There are so many working guitarists in Spain and elsewhere whose accomplishments may never gain wide recognition, yet it is they who make up the basis of the living art that is Flamenco today.

¡Viva el Arte!

Juan Martín.

THE CASSETTE and CD RECORDING
Music composed and played by Juan Martín.
Narration spoken by Sr. I. Montañana.
Recorded by EMI Ltd.

THE BOOK
Photographs (except back cover), transcriptions into
musical notation and cifra, text and design by P. Campbell.
Typesetting and artwork by Dahling Dahling Ltd.,
D'Arblay House, 10a Poland Street, London W.1.
Printed by Halstan & Co. Ltd., Amersham, Bucks.

OTHER ALBUMS OF JUAN MARTÍN'S MUSIC PUBLISHED BY
UNITED MUSIC PUBLISHERS LTD.

THE EXCITING SOUND OF FLAMENCO
(Vol. I)

ZAMBRA MORA and
BRISAS HABANERAS

THE EXCITING SOUND OF FLAMENCO
(Vol. II)

MI RUMBA and
AIRES GADITANOS (Cantiñas)

Published in musical notation and cifra.

A stereo recording by Juan Martín of both volumes of The Exciting Sound of Flamenco is available on cassette either from United Music Publishers Ltd., or from:

FLAMENCOVISION
P.O. Box 508
London N3 3SY

SOLO RECORDINGS

The following flamenco guitar recordings by Juan Martín are currently available through various distributors.
Further information from FLAMENCOVISION as above.

The Andalucia Suites Flamencovision FV01
Luna Negra Flamencovision FV02

Both recordings are available in CD and cassette form.

Juan Martín's "La Guitarra Flamenca" video series
(three one-hour videos, each with 150 page book in notation and cifra)
Warner Chappell Music Ltd., distributed by IMP (International Music Publications Limited)

THE CASSETTE/CD

Music composed and played by **JUAN MARTÍN**

WRITING DOWN FLAMENCO

Flamenco is an art-form which traditionally does not use written notation. Many readers must, therefore, wonder about the authenticity and accuracy of the transcriptions of Juan Martín's music into staff notation and tablature *(cifra)*. The approach adopted here was designed to preserve as much as possible the vital spontaneity of Juan's playing and to avoid simplification or distortion in showing how Flamenco is actually played.

After the main outlines of the Method had been decided upon, he played and tape-recorded the pieces *impromptu*, most of them in just one very inspired session. In this way he linked together many melodic *falsetas* and rhythmic passages of *rasgueo* into pieces suitable for a progressive introduction to guitar techniques as well as for solo performance. Next, the music was transcribed from the tape-recording into notation and *cifra*. Some further sections were recorded and transcribed separately in order to complete the coverage of basic techniques and essential *toques*. Working now from the basis of the transcriptions and the recordings, Juan memorised the pieces as he had originally played them and re-recorded them for the cassette to go with the book. Both during and after this re-recording at EMI's studios the transcriptions were checked through again note by note to ensure that they correspond as exactly as possible to the final recording you will hear.   P.C.

'ELEMENTS OF FLAMENCO'

The pupil who learns with Juan Martín receives much more than just a personal initiation into flamenco music and guitar-playing. He is also introduced to a whole world of Flamenco as Juan emphasises and demonstrates the essential musical values which give the music its unique strength and appeal. In order to convey these more theoretical aspects of his teaching the book includes, among the sections called 'Elements of Flamenco', discussions of key terms used in Flamenco and a brief outline of the history of the art, along with other, more practical details about the guitar. These sections, listed below, are presented separately at the end of the earlier Lessons in the book.

THE BOOK   Contents

1.1 The traditional flamenco way of holding the guitar, supported on the right thigh.

LESSON 1 Getting Started

Tuning the guitar

The flamenco position

Introduction to rasgueo

A first-day solo

> The musical illustrations recorded on the cassette follow the sequence of the printed text. The symbol  indicates points in the text at which it is appropriate to switch on your recorder to hear the next item on the tape. Each item is introduced by a brief announcement on the recording and is also named in the text.

In this first lesson we start by learning to tune the guitar. We then look at how to sit and hold the instrument in the proper flamenco position, and from there you can quickly progress to playing flamenco *rasgueos* and a short sequence of a *Malagueña*.

The only assumption at this point is that you have a Spanish type of guitar with nylon strings.

You do not need a special flamenco instrument to begin with, so the question of how to choose the right sort of guitar is left until further on in the book (p. 50). Buying an expensive guitar before you know what to look for and what sort suits you best can turn out to be a costly mistake. Better, therefore, to make a start with even a very modest instrument before you commit yourself to major expense.

If your guitar is not already fitted with *golpeadores* (tapping-plates) you will need to buy some self-adhesive ones from a guitar shop, but they are not necessary for the first lesson. Once fitted, they may not be removed easily without risk of damage to the surface of the guitar.

Flamenco guitarists traditionally do not read music but learn by imitation and by ear. You, too, will not need to understand musical notation to learn the music in this book. Other simpler methods of representing the music recorded on the cassette will show you what to play. If you do want to learn notation, however, Appendix A contains a brief introduction to the subject.

Tuning the guitar

We begin by tuning the 5th string, which is the middle one of the three bass strings wound with a covering of wire, to the note A. This note is heard as a continuous tone at the very start of the cassette.

Adjust the machine-head or tuning-peg (see photo 1.2) to bring the 5th string to the right degree of tension, so that when the string is plucked it sounds exactly the same note as the A note on the cassette. Once you have achieved this, you can use the 5th string as the basis for tuning all the other strings, as is described in detail on page 2.

At first you may find it difficult to be sure when two notes (initially the note on the cassette and the note of the 5th string and, later, notes on different strings) are exactly the same. Practice, however, will make you more confident about doing this accurately. If it sounds right then it probably is right.

The quickest method for tuning any string is to tighten it progressively so that you always tune upwards in pitch towards the correct pitch, rather than downwards by slackening the string. If you overtighten so that the string sounds sharp, that is higher in pitch than the exact note you are aiming for, loosen it off just enough to let you approach the right note from a lower (flat) pitch by tightening the string again.

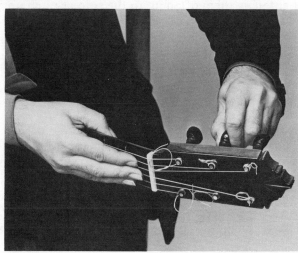

CASSETTE: INITIAL TUNING TONE, A

1.2 Adjusting a tuning-peg. Right hand braces the neck of the guitar.

For the beginner: details of tuning

The basic method of tuning, starting from the 5th string, can be summarised by a diagram. The dots show at which frets the strings must be pressed against the fingerboard to obtain the note to which the next higher 'open' string is tuned.

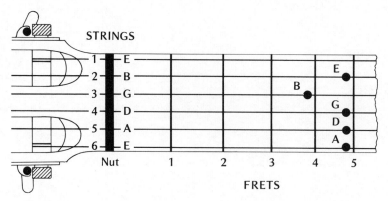

When the 5th string is stopped at the fifth fret, it gives the note D to which the 4th string is to be tuned. To 'stop' the 5th string at the correct fret, a finger of the left hand presses it firmly against the fingerboard behind the fifth fret. The fingertip should be immediately next to, but not on top of, the fifth fret on the side nearer the machine-heads or pegs. Sound the note by plucking the string with a finger or thumb of the right hand and then tighten the 4th string until it produces exactly the same note.

Repeat the same procedure on the now tuned 4th string to find the note, G, for the 3rd string. The note is made by stopping the 4th string at the fifth fret.

The next step is different. To find the note, B, to which the 2nd string is tuned the 3rd string is stopped at the fourth fret — not the fifth fret this time. For all other adjoining pairs of strings the difference in pitch (the 'interval') between them is five semitones, equivalent to five fret spaces, but between the 3rd and 2nd strings it is only four semitones.

The note for the 1st string, E, is found by stopping the 2nd string at the fifth fret.

To tune the 6th string to its note of bass E, the lowest note on the guitar, you need to make the note from this string when it is stopped at the fifth fret the same as the note of the open (i.e. not stopped) 5th string, the A we started from on the cassette. This is slightly more complicated than for the other strings because the 6th string has to be stopped before a note on it can be compared with the same note on another string.

If you have any doubts about the correctness of the tuning, recheck each string in turn against the adjoining ones. Also, the E of the 1st string should be exactly two octaves higher than the E of the 6th. Once you have learned to play chords you will find it helpful to check the tuning further by playing the main chord or chords in the piece you are about to play to hear whether they sound absolutely right.

New strings will quickly lose their pitch as they stretch when first put on the guitar. You will need to keep tightening them often up to the correct pitch until they settle at a stable intonation after a few days.

To get the best sound from your guitar and the right tension in the strings, the strings should not only be in tune relative to each other but should also be at the correct 'concert' pitch overall. The tuning note at the beginning of the cassette will start you off, but soon you will need a pitch-pipe or tuning fork so that you can tune anywhere, unless you have a very good memory for pitch. An A tuning fork will give the pitch of the first string stopped at the fifth fret, and a C one the note at its eighth fret.

Notes of the open strings in musical notation

The strings of the guitar, ascending from bass 6th to treble 1st, are tuned to the notes E A D G B E. In musical notation for the guitar these are written as follows:

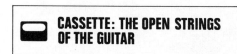

CASSETTE: THE OPEN STRINGS OF THE GUITAR

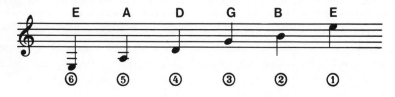

It is a convention that guitar music is written in the treble clef an octave higher than it actually sounds. If you were tuning a guitar from a piano, therefore, the notes of the strings as written for the piano would be:

For the more advanced player: further aids to accurate tuning

To obtain maximum accuracy in tuning, the use of natural harmonics can supplement the basic method already outlined. These pure, bell-like notes are produced when the whole string is vibrated in a special kind of way, in fractions of its total length. This is done by lightly touching, but not stopping, the string exactly over an appropriate fret and then lifting the touching finger away at the moment the string is plucked by a finger of the right hand. If, for example, the string is touched this way by a left hand finger exactly over the 12th fret, which lies midway along its length from nut to bridge, the string is vibrated in halves, so that the harmonic produced sounds an octave higher than the open string. (An alternative method of playing harmonics is to touch the string with the right index finger over the appropriate fret and to pluck it with the right thumb, lifting the index away at the instant the string is sounded).

When the guitar is in tune, the harmonic sounded when the touching finger is placed over the fifth fret on the 6th string is the same note as the harmonic sounded on the 5th string when it is touched over the seventh fret. A similar relationship holds for the next two adjacent pairs of strings. Then, after checking the tuning of the lower four strings in relation to each other in this way, the B of the open 2nd string is obtained from the B harmonic sounded by touching over the seventh fret on the 6th string. The E of the open 1st string is obtained from the E harmonic sounded with the touching finger over the seventh fret of the 5th string.

The final test should still be to check the sound of the chords of the piece you are going to play.

Holding the guitar: the flamenco position

The traditional flamenco way of holding the guitar is to support its weight on the right thigh. This is very different from the 'classical' position, which is not suitable for Flamenco. Try to imitate the position demonstrated in the photographs as closely as you can, and check your position by sitting in front of a mirror, preferably a full-length one.

Posture

First you need a chair without arms, of the right height for your legs. It should allow your thighs to be parallel to the floor or, better still, slightly inclined with the knees rather higher from the floor than the hip-joints, so that the guitar can be securely balanced. If the thighs slope at all the other way, that is downwards from hips to knees, the guitar may tend to slide forwards. Place the feet, which may be together or slightly apart, so as to get maximum height of the knees from the floor. The knees are relaxed and allowed to incline outwards. Keep the back as straight and upright as possible, in a relaxed posture to avoid strain. The shoulders stay square and level. The basic posture is shown in photo 1.1.

1.3 Holding the guitar on right thigh, balanced entirely by weight of right arm.

Balancing the guitar

The larger curve of the guitar is now placed on the right thigh, usually on the outer side of the thigh. The right upper arm rests on top of the guitar as shown in photo 1.3, the pressure downwards of the weight of the relaxed arm being all that is required to balance the guitar at the correct angle. Neck and shoulder muscles should stay relaxed. Gravity alone maintains the position of the guitar.

To bring the right hand into the playing position, the forearm is raised by bending the arm at the elbow until the hand, which stays relaxed, lies over the strings of the guitar between soundhole and bridge, as shown in photo 1.4.

1.4 Right hand brought into basic playing position.

As shown in photo 1.5, in which the left hand is shown stopping the strings, the back of the guitar should be just about vertical to the floor. Its neck is inclined slightly forwards, away from the left side of the body. This brings the neck into a position comfortable for the left hand and also limits the extent to which the back of the guitar is pressed against the chest. The back of the instrument must not be muffled since it reflects the sound and projects it forwards.

To summarise, 4 main points should be kept in mind while you are getting used to the flamenco way of holding the guitar:

1. The weight of the guitar is in no way supported by the left hand, which must be completely unencumbered in its movements.

2. There is a gap between guitar and chest.

3. Your back should be straight with shoulders level.

4. The whole posture should be as relaxed and tension-free as possible.

1.5 Neck of guitar inclined forwards away from left side of chest. Note straightness of the spine.

People vary in the ease with which they can manage to hold the guitar in this position to start with. You are quite likely to believe, the first few times you try it, that it is going to be impossible to balance the guitar securely without it slipping about. But like everybody else you will be able to master it with perseverance. Keep trying to play in this position at all times. If you have very great difficulty, however, and are beginning to despair, you may have to lower the guitar so that the hollow between the two curves of the body of the guitar rests on your right thigh. But keep trying the flamenco position so that you can gain greater comfort and confidence in it. The logic of it lies in the straight posture it allows the spine, the strength and control it gives to the right hand and the ease of access for the left hand in playing at frets high up the neck of the guitar.

You may see flamenco guitarists varying the position of holding the guitar, sometimes even changing while playing. But it is important not to complicate things at this stage: other positions will be described later. The ability to play in the traditional flamenco position is a must for every flamenco player.

Two chords

With the guitar now tuned and in position, we can bring both hands into play by learning two important chords, E major and A minor. These chords are played here with all six strings of the guitar, helping you to familiarise yourself with the richness and strength of sound your instrument can produce.

 CASSETTE: EXERCISE 1

Listen to Exercise 1 on the cassette and you will hear four beats of the chord of E major alternating with four beats of A minor, played with down-strokes of the right thumb. Before you try to play this we will look at what is required of each hand in turn.

E major: the left hand

Photos 1.6 and 1.7 show the position taken up by the left hand fingers for the chord of E major. The position can be represented by a chord diagram, which is simply a diagram of the strings and frets with the number corresponding to each circular dot showing which finger is placed where:

The fingers of the left hand are indicated by numbers as follows:

    1 = index finger

    2 = middle finger

    3 = third or ring finger

    4 = little finger

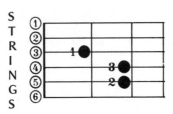

E major chord diagram

1.6 E major chord position from above.

The E major chord can be represented in musical notation as follows:

Numbers alongside the dots of the notes again show which finger of the left hand stops a string to make the corresponding note. The 0's indicate that the notes which they are adjacent to are made on open strings.

Try to copy the way the fingers are placed in the photos, noting, if you can, the points mentioned in the caption.

Watching the left hand fingers

To place the fingers of the left hand behind the correct frets when you have the guitar in position you will need to look at them over the top of the guitar. There will be a temptation to pull the left hand nearer your body in order to get a better view, but you should resist this, since it will bring the back of the guitar against the chest. The plane of the front surface of the guitar stays upright or nearly so. See photo 1.5.

The right hand

To sound the chord, strike firmly downwards towards the floor across the strings with a deliberate sweep of the right thumb. The fleshy edge of the tip of the thumb contacts all six strings in rapid succession. The movement of the thumb is shown in photos 1.8 (a) and (b).

Repeat the movement to produce a slow steady rhythm.

1.7 (above) Left hand position for E major chord. Fingers 1, 3, 2 stop the strings. The fingertips are close to the frets without pressing down on top of them and are nearly at right angles to the fretboard. The knuckles of the left hand are parallel to the edge of the fretboard. The wrist is in a relaxed posture.

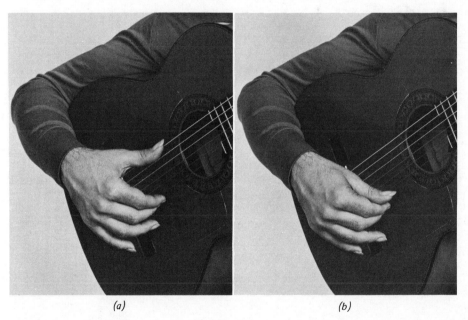

(a)   (b)

1.8 (left) Downwards sweep of the thumb across all six strings.
 (a) start of stroke.
 (b) end of stroke.

A minor

Photo 1.9 shows the position of the left hand fingers for the chord of A minor, shown in chord-diagram form as:

and in notation as:

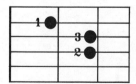

A minor chord diagram

You will see that the fingers are in exactly the same formation relative to each other as in the preceding chord of E major. The only difference is that they stop strings 4, 3 and 2 instead of 5, 4 and 3.

Sound the chord with downstrokes of the thumb, repeating them in rhythm as before.

1.9 Chord position of A minor.

Changing chords

Having learned to play the chords of E major and A minor, your next step is to be able to change smoothly from one to the other.

Start by playing repeated thumbstrokes on the E major chord in a slow and regular rhythm. Beating time with your left foot will help to keep the rhythm even. When you have got the rhythm going steadily, move all three left hand fingers holding down the chord across together to take up the position of the A minor chord. The fingers move as one since, as already noted, the two chords use the fingers in identical formation. You will need to play very slowly at first so that there is no detectable delay in the rhythm as you change chords.

Having changed to A minor, keep the rhythm going as before with the thumbstrokes and then, when you feel ready for it, change back to E major, again without holding up the pulse of the rhythm. Keep doing this again and again until you can change chords easily.

You can now proceed to play Exercise 1, which is simply four beats of E major alternating with four of A minor. Counting aloud will help you make the change-over at the right moments. Written out in chord diagrams and notation, Exercise 1 looks like this:

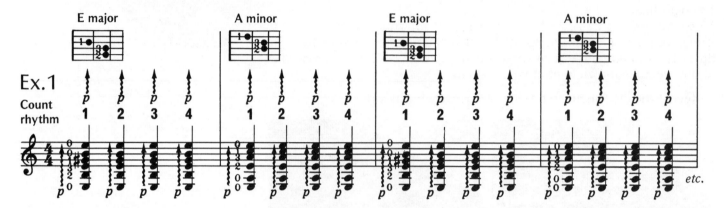

Some symbols

To indicate the kind of thumbstroke just described, the exercise above uses the symbol ⬍.

A stroke by thumb or finger of the right hand moving from bass to treble downwards towards the floor is called a 'downstroke' and is shown by an arrow, ↑ . In notation the arrow refers to the chord which immediately follows it. An arrow in the opposite direction, ↓ , is a stroke from treble to bass, an 'upstroke'.

At first sight, you might think that these arrows look the wrong way round, but you will easily avoid any confusion by relating them to the guitar, as shown in the diagram *(right)*.

The arrows are drawn the way they are because of the order in which the strings are struck: in notation the higher notes are nearer the top of the page than the lower.

A wavy arrow, ⬍ , means that the chord is played in a spread-out way, with the individual strings heard in quick succession. The straight arrow is used where the stroke is made so rapidly that the sound is a single beat.

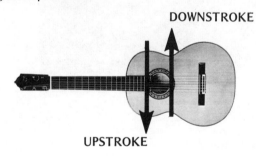

DOWNSTROKE

UPSTROKE

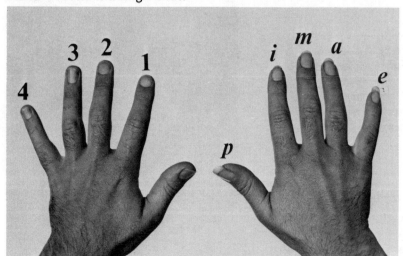

1.10 Symbols for the fingers of right and left hands.

The letter beneath each arrow shows which finger of the right hand makes the stroke. Here it is **p** for *pulgar* (thumb).

Other letters used in the book are:

    a for *añular* (ring or 3rd finger)

    m for *medio* (middle or 2nd finger)

    i for *indice* (index or 1st finger)

    e for *meñique* (little or 4th finger)

p, **a**, **m** and **i** are standard symbols widely used in guitar music. Use of the 4th finger (in *rasgueos*) is special to Flamenco and there is no standard symbol.

Introducing RASGUEO

Switch on the cassette to listen to Exercises 2, 3 and 4. These demonstrate your next objective, which is to play the E major chord using flamenco *'rasgueo'*, the exciting sound most characteristic of the flamenco guitar. The exercises will be discussed step by step.

CASSETTE: EXERCISES 2, 3 and 4

The word *'rasgueo'*, which embraces all strumming techniques using one or more fingers of the right hand, is pronounced 'rachayo' in the language of Flamenco, with the 'ch' guttural as in the Scottish 'loch'. *'Rasgueado'* (from the verb *rasguear*) is an alternative term.

Here we meet two of the commonest kinds of *rasgueo*, the single stroke with the index finger and the longer roll of the 4-stroke *rasgueo*.

Index finger RASGUEO

(i) **Downstrokes.** Place the right hand in the position shown in photo 1.11(a), with the thumb resting lightly beside the sound-hole of the guitar on the rosette. This stabilises the hand, which stays relaxed. Flex the index finger from the knuckle so that its nail nearly touches the base of the thumb. From this position flick it forwards, striking downwards across all six strings to reach the position shown in photo 1.11(b). The movement is as if you were flicking a small object lying on the 6th string across the strings to just beyond the 1st. Do it quite gently to start with. The line of movement of the stroke is straight across the strings, at right angles to them.

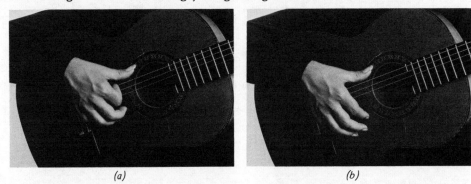

1.11 Index finger downstroke — thumb resting on rosette of guitar (for index stroke across all six strings).
    (a) start of stroke.
    (b) end of stroke.

(a)   (b)

Do it again and again in a slow steady rhythm, beating time with your foot. With practice you will achieve a shorter, crisper sound. Exercise 2 can now be written as follows: count the rhythm aloud in 6's this time rather than 4's.

CASSETTE: EXERCISE 2

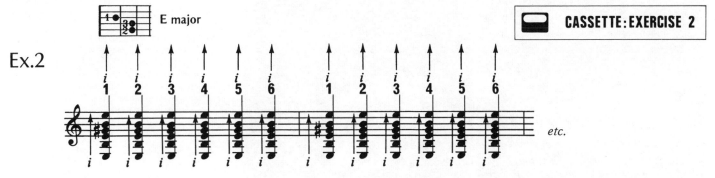

Ex.2

(ii) **Upstrokes.** Once you have started the rhythm going steadily with downstrokes of the index finger you can begin to introduce upstrokes after each downstroke. On each upstroke the index flicks back towards its position at the start of the downstroke [shown in 1.11(a)], hitting the higher-pitched strings so that only the first four (strings 1, 2, 3 and 4) are sounded. You should try to get a 'spring' in the movement in order to give crispness and an elastic sort of 'bounce' to the rhythm of alternate down- and upstrokes heard in Exercise 3 and written as:

CASSETTE: EXERCISE 3

Ex.3

The 4-stroke RASGUEO

This very important technique (shown in sequence in photos 1.12 and 1.13) consists of a rapid succession of down-strokes by the four fingers of the right hand, in the order **e, a, m, i**. The hand position is the same basic position shown in 1.11, except that the thumb now rests on the sixth string without touching the front surface of the guitar, instead of resting on the rosette. The thumb adopts this position to stabilise the hand in playing *rasgueo* when, as here, only the top five strings are to be sounded.

The fingers are first flexed so that they nearly, but not quite, touch the palm. Each finger in turn is uncurled so that it hits the strings, brushing downwards across them with the same sort of movement just described for the index downstroke. You can start by doing this slowly and gently. Try to get an even succession of strokes by the four fingers so that each is heard distinctly. Each finger moves independently of the others and you should try to give each equal force, although this will be hard initially with **e** and **a**. Resist any temptation to push downwards with the whole hand so that the fingers are dragged across the strings. Hand and wrist are stationary and very relaxed.

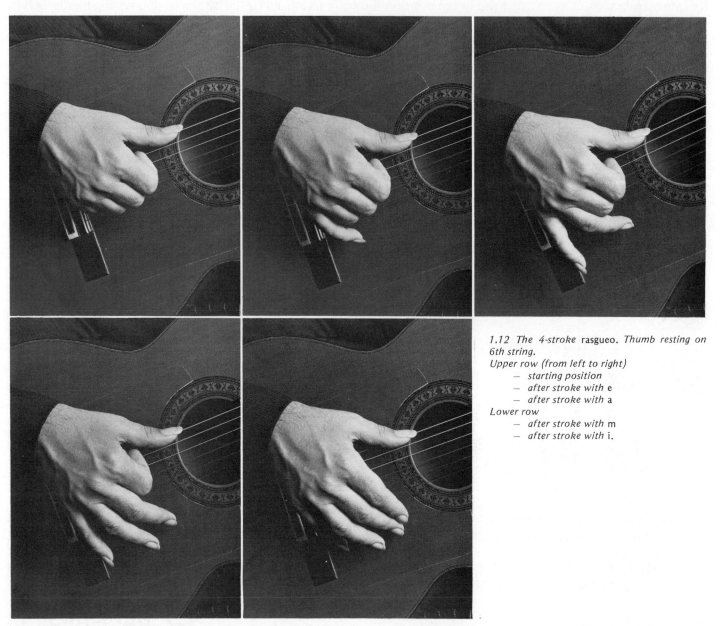

1.12 The 4-stroke rasgueo. *Thumb resting on 6th string.*
Upper row (from left to right)
    — *starting position*
    — *after stroke with* e
    — *after stroke with* a
Lower row
    — *after stroke with* m
    — *after stroke with* i.

Practising the 4-stroke RASGUEO without a guitar

You can build up facility and strength by practising this *rasgueo* at any time, at home, at work, on the bus. To do this, flex the fingers so that their nails do actually press into the palm of the right hand, then flick each out separately in the order **e a m i** against the resistance provided by the ball and base of the thumb. Alternatively you can balance the thumb on the top or edge of a table, the side of your thigh, your seat on the bus, and then use the surface or edge as the resistance against which you flick the fingers.

The important thing is to learn to control each finger at a time, making the separate stroke of each equally powerful. With continued practice you should be able to repeat the sequence **e a m i e a m i** etc. in a smooth un-broken rhythm without pause between the **i** of one *rasgueo* and the **e** of the next. Once you can do this you have the basis for longer or continuous rolls on the guitar.

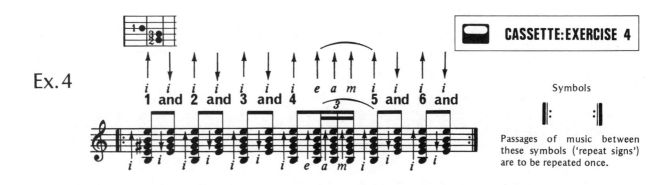

Ex. 4

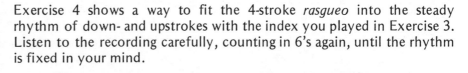

Symbols

$\|\!:$ $:\!\|$

Passages of music between these symbols ('repeat signs') are to be repeated once.

Exercise 4 shows a way to fit the 4-stroke *rasgueo* into the steady rhythm of down- and upstrokes with the index you played in Exercise 3. Listen to the recording carefully, counting in 6's again, until the rhythm is fixed in your mind.

Note that the upstroke after beat 4 is left out. Instead, at the instant you would have played it, the 4-stroke *rasgueo* starts with the stroke by the little finger, **e**. **e, a** and **m** strokes then take up the duration of half a beat so that the fourth stroke, with **i**, carries the accent of the *rasgueo* on beat 5. You can treat this stroke with the index just like the previous index downstrokes on the beat and follow it with an index upstroke before the next downstroke on beat 6. The right thumb rests lightly on the 6th string throughout.

Notation of RASGUEO

In this book the *rasgueos* are written out in full, with the stroke of each finger represented by a separate arrow placed immediately to the left of the chord each finger sounds.

This method shows clearly where the accent falls, and in the 4-stroke *rasgueo* it indicates accurately that the movement of each finger is important and distinct. It will also allow the exact representation of other and more complicated *rasgueos*.

In the exercise above the 4-stroke *rasgueo* with accent on the final downstroke with the index is shown as follows:

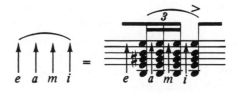

Upstrokes with the index finger usually hit fewer strings than downstrokes. This was shown in the notation for Exercise 3 by giving 6 notes to the downstrokes and only 4 (sounded by the top four strings) to the upstrokes.

You do not need to become too obsessional about exactly how many strings each finger hits. In the case of the downstroke it is usually important that it begins from the correct bass string. With upstrokes, on the other hand, the impact of the stroke will fall mainly on the higher-pitched strings and sometimes only on the 1st and 2nd.

1.13 The 4-stroke rasgueo. *Sometimes, to give the stroke of each finger extra emphasis (as well as for practice purposes), the fingers are pressed into the palm and are then flicked out in turn. The bottom photo shows how the index is flicked out against the thumb.*

9

Exercise 5 uses exactly the same right hand movements as the preceding exercise, but combines it with the left hand chord change of Exercise 1. 6 beats of E major alternate with 6 of A minor. Again, there should be no interruption in the rhythm as you change chords from one to the other.

Ex. 5

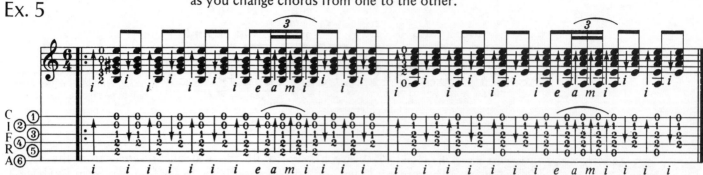

CIFRA: Besides being written in notation, Exercise 5 is shown in *cifra* (Spanish for 'cipher'). This method of tablature will be used throughout the book as an alternative to conventional musical notation for those who do not read music and as a supplement for those who do.

The six horizontal lines represent the six strings of the guitar, as shown by the numbers at their left hand ends. The numbers on the lines are those of the frets (not the fingers) behind which the strings are to be stopped by fingers of the left hand. In order to find which finger is used you can refer to the numbers alongside the notes in the notation above, but they can, in any case, be worked out from the way the frets required fall most naturally under the fingers. A nought, 0, indicates that the string is played open.

The value of the *cifra* system will become clearer in the next piece.

The notation of time-values
The duration of individual notes in the music can be heard from the cassette. Time-values are indicated in the musical notation but they have not been duplicated in the *cifra* in order not to clutter the page. The right hand fingering for strokes of *rasgueos*, however, is indicated in both the notation and the *cifra*.

A first-day solo: Malagueña

With the chords of E major and A minor as the basis, it is easy to play a theme from the traditional flamenco song of Málaga, the Malagueña. Play the piece first on the cassette before we examine it step by step.

The recording is of the whole piece played at full speed first, followed by two much slower renderings to help you learn its structure.

The first step is to play the basic melody with the thumb on 4th, 3rd and 2nd strings. Start by placing the first and second fingers of the left hand in position on just 3rd and 4th strings for a chord of E major, as shown on the right:

The right thumb now sounds the 4th, 3rd and 2nd strings in sequence. Its movement is a single downward stroke which sounds the 4th string, pauses momentarily after coming to rest against the 3rd string, then follows through to sound the 3rd string and then the 2nd string after a similar pause. Repeat these three notes once, as follows:

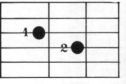

E major

1.14 Left hand position for E major chord using top 4 strings only.

The inclined arrow p denotes a followed-through stroke by the thumb, hitting in turn an ascending sequence of strings.

Next, move the left hand fingers to an A minor position on strings 2 and 3.

Strike these two strings with a single stroke and follow-through of the thumb as before. Then with the thumb strike each of the following notes in turn: open 2nd string (after lifting the 1st finger), 3rd string stopped by 2 at the second fret, open 3rd string (after lifting the second finger), then 4th string stopped by 3 at the 3rd fret.

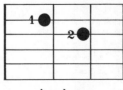

A minor

1.15 A minor on top 3 strings.

Go back to repeat the whole sequence, finally sounding the open 6th string. In music and *cifra*, the sequence so far can be shown as:

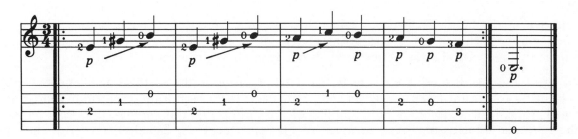

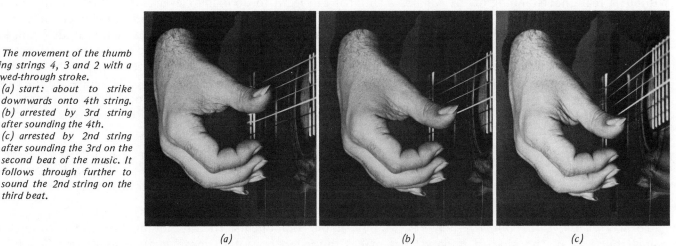

1.16 The movement of the thumb striking strings 4, 3 and 2 with a followed-through stroke.
(a) start: about to strike downwards onto 4th string.
(b) arrested by 3rd string after sounding the 4th.
(c) arrested by 2nd string after sounding the 3rd on the second beat of the music. It follows through further to sound the 2nd string on the third beat.

Now repeat the whole sequence again, this time plucking the open 1st string with the first finger of the right hand in the gap after each thumbstroke.

At the end, after playing the open 6th string, add a 4-stroke *rasgueo* on E major, timing it so that its accent falls on the beat. The final chord which follows is a downstroke made with the index or, if you can, middle and ring fingers of the right hand (**m, a**) simultaneously. The movement of the two fingers together is performed in the same way as the downstroke with the index already described; using these two fingers together gives a more emphatic stroke. It is a very flamenco technique which you will meet again later on in the book. Try it with the index stroke first.

The piece is written out in full below. Play the cassette recording again before trying to play it all the way through with the alternation of thumb and index in strictly regular rhythm.

Malagueña

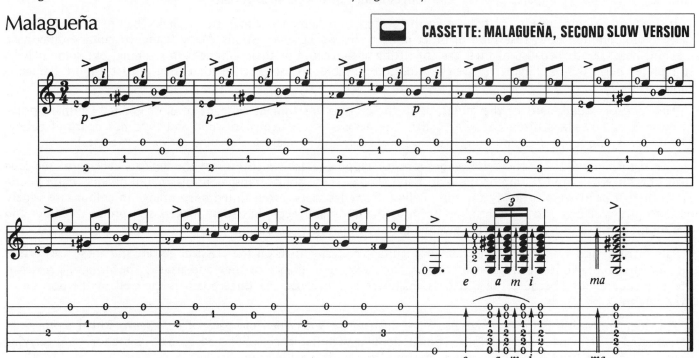

Elements of Flamenco 1   Compás   The Guitar

COMPÁS

The basic element of rhythm in Flamenco is called the *compás*, a word which literally means 'compass' and hence a 'measure' of music. Each *compás* is a recurring pattern of accented beats which gives the regular pulse of the rhythm its impetus and metrical form. Different kinds of *compás* have different patterns.

Repeated again and again, the patterns create that vital pulsation in the rhythms of Flamenco which is like a heart-beat, bringing to life their expressiveness and excitement. If you can learn, even from your very first steps with the guitar, to aim for a profound understanding of the various types of *compás*, then you can soon begin to generate the rhythmic impetus on which so much of Flamenco depends. Establish a sense of the *compás* deep within you and the guitar will come alive in your hands: ignore it or lose the pulse of it and the music dies at once. Without a real understanding of the *compás* a guitarist can learn to do many clever and even very difficult things on the guitar, but his playing will never come to life as Flamenco. He may 'understand' the *compás* in the sense that he knows the theory about the ways the beats of the rhythm are structured and accented in different kinds of pattern, but a feeling for the *compás* ultimately demands something much more than an intellectual awareness if one is to communicate its physical energy and momentum. It has to become a part of one's whole being, an inner bodily sense that is translated into musical expression through the movements of the hands and the fingers. This kind of physical identification with the rhythms of Flamenco comes fairly readily to some people. More often, however, it has to be worked for with patient persistence by continual self-awareness as one plays and by absorbing as much Flamenco as one can, in all its forms.

The ability to play the *compás* strictly and unerringly is the main yardstick by which all a guitarist's efforts will be appraised by the expert. You may be sure that the *aficionado* (devotee) of Flamenco will quickly dismiss your playing as being of little interest if you play *fuera de compás*, (out of *compás*), no matter how elaborate and speedy your technique.

To play *a compás* (in *compás*), then, has two inseparable components. The rhythm must generate a compellingly regular pulse to it, the kind of impetus that makes the listener want to move in time to the music. Also, the accentuation of beats and the number of beats in each musical phrase must at all times fit the characteristic pattern of the particular rhythmic form being played. These different forms are called *toques* and we shall meet the most central of them, the Soleares, in Lesson 2. The *compás* is strictly adhered to not only in the passages of rhythmic strumming *(rasqueo)* but also in the passages of melody which are called *falsetas*.

The flamenco guitar

The flamenco guitar shares many points of similarity in construction with the 'classical' Spanish guitar, but there are important differences. The sides and back are of light-coloured Spanish cypress rather than the dark *palo santo* (Brazilian rosewood) of the finest classical models. This, combined with slightly different wood thicknesses, internal strutting and dimensions, gives the flamenco guitar its characteristic tone, a more penetrating brilliance and vibrancy of response compared to the mellower resonance of the classical guitar.

Instead of machine-heads for tightening the strings, the flamenco guitar traditionally has pegs of ebony or, sadly more common now, rosewood or other more easily worked hardwoods. Many flamenco guitars today have machine-heads, both because of their ease of fitting and because of their simplicity for tuning, but some players still prefer pegs: they are lighter in weight and more durable, and some claim that they impart a more flamenco tone.

The *tapa* or soundboard of the guitar, as in the classical instrument, is made of close-grained German spruce *(pinabete)* or nowadays often Canadian cedar. The neck is of cedar or hardwood and the fingerboard of ebony. The bridge is *palo santo*. Nut and bridge-saddle are of bone and in Spanish are called the *huesos* (bones).

The flamenco guitar is fitted with *golpeadores* or tapping-plates which protect the delicate surface of the *tapa* from the fingernails and thumb of the right hand. Today these are of transparent plastic but opaque white plastic or mother of pearl were formerly the rule. Polyurethane lacquers, often tinted deep orange in colour, are widely used to give a strong and brilliant gloss finish to the body and neck, but some makers still prefer the older and less robust spirit varnishes which often give the guitar a much paler colouring.

The 'action' and response of the flamenco guitar are faster than on the classical guitar, and these are further factors which contribute to its special capacity for a ringing brilliance of tone and attack. The strings lie closer to the fingerboard both because the bridge is shallower and because the fingerboard is inclined in the portion of overlying the *tapa*.

A recent innovation is the *'guitarra negra'*, an instrument with sides and back of *palo santo* which is otherwise constructed to flamenco specifications. Though popular with flamenco soloists because of its big tone and carrying power, it lacks the brightness and earthy intensity of the traditional instrument.

THE FLAMENCO GUITAR

Flamenco guitar with tuning-pegs.

Flamenco guitar with machine-heads.

HEEL *(Tacón)*

SIDE *(Aro)*

HEAD *(Cabeza)*

TUNING-PEGS *(Clavijas)*

NUT *(Hueso)*

STRINGS *(Cuerdas)*

FRETS *(Trastes)*

NECK *(Mastil)*

FINGERBOARD OR FRETBOARD *(Diapasón)*

SOUNDBOARD *(Tapa)*

ROSETTE *(Embocadura)*

SOUNDHOLE *(Boca)*

TAPPING-PLATE *(Golpeador)*

BRIDGE-SADDLE *(Hueso)*

BRIDGE *(Puente)*

PURFLING *(Fileteria)*

Strings

The three lower strings of the flamenco guitar, the 'basses', i.e. 6th, 5th and 4th, are made of nylon floss wound with fine metal wire. The third (G) string is of plain nylon filament or may be nylon floss wound with nylon filament; the latter type is thicker and its sound tends to have longer 'sustain', but it wears out more quickly than the plain filament. The second string may be similarly covered with a winding of nylon, though it is usually plain. The first string is nearly always of plain nylon filament but one or two brands provide a covered first. Some makes of plain nylon strings have a smooth surface. Others are slightly opaque and rougher to the touch from being milled to provide a perfectly round cross-section and more even intonation.

Normal and high tension strings are suitable for the flamenco guitar and individual tastes differ. Sometimes you may find it best to combine trebles of one tension with basses of a different tension in order to obtain the best balance of sound and action from your guitar. There are excellent strings by Savarez, Darco, La Bella and D'Addario to choose from. After extensive experiment and with the collaboration of John D'Addario a special set of flamenco strings has been produced, called 'JUAN MARTÍN FLAMENCO DE CONCIERTO'. These strings can definitely give a flamenco quality to even a dull-sounding guitar.

Care of the guitar

When not in use the guitar should be protected by a rigid, well-fitting case. It is a good idea to leave the guitar out of its case a little at times to let it 'breathe'. Extremes of temperature and humidity must be avoided. Central-heating can be very damaging to guitars and if the guitar has to be kept in a centrally heated room, humidification of the air is strongly advisable to avoid the risk of cracking and warping. This is especially likely to occur if the guitar is made of inadequately seasoned wood. The great *guitarreros* use wood that is many years old to ensure that it is fully dried out, but cheaper instruments are often made of much more recently felled timber.

After use, a duster or soft cloth should be used to wipe the strings and can be used with care on the wooden surfaces. Do not use polishes or other potions, otherwise the delicate finish of the guitar may suffer and the wood may absorb them. A very slightly moistened cloth should be capable of removing grease spots and other marks.

Small cracks in the face or sides of the wood may be of little consequence. They are not uncommon in fine guitars which have been much played. Before they attain considerable size, however, the attention of a skilled repairer should be sought. Any warping of the fingerboard is of much more serious import and will demand expert and costly repair.

Care of the strings

Cleaning the strings by wiping with a cloth after playing prevents early deterioration from perspiration. Covered strings may be given prolonged life if they are reversed end to end when their brilliance begins to fade. One can wash strings to give them a still longer life but their recovery is so short-lived after this procedure as to be hardly worthwhile.

When the strings are changed it is essential to do this one at a time so that the tension of the soundboard is not left slackened off for long periods. It is a useful idea, however, occasionally to slacken off all the covered strings (but not the plain trebles) for brief periods of perhaps up to five minutes and then to tighten them again after wiping the strings with a cloth; this procedure gives the tone renewed brilliance.

The left-handed player

It might seem logical for the left-handed player to reverse the hand positions and order of stringing of the guitar so that he strikes the strings with the left hand. This has to be an individual decision, but it must be remembered that if a high quality guitar is going to be wanted one day, it may need to be made specially. This is because the internal construction of the *tapa* is not fully symmetrical and interchanging the treble and bass strings on a normal right-handed instrument will spoil the tone.

The CEJILLA

The *cejilla* is a device which is fixed across the strings to raise their pitch. It effectively acts as a movable nut which stops the strings when tightly fixed immediately behind a fret. Originally used to allow the guitar tuning to be adjusted easily to the key of the singer's voice in the *Cante*, it is now used for almost all performances of Flamenco to give added brightness to the guitar by pitching it in a higher key.

For solo playing the *cejilla* is usually placed at a fret between 1 and 4, commonly at the 2nd fret. Fret-positions for the *cejilla* higher than 4 should generally only be used for accompaniment.

In order to develop strength and technical facility in the left hand it is advisable to practise exercises without the *cejilla* in place; the hand has to work harder, especially in the stretch, in the first position than in the higher positions.

Two main types of *cejilla* are available. The traditional form is made of hardwood, often finely carved and decorated. It is tied down by means of a nylon string which is wound round a wooden peg inserted in a hole in the wooden cross-piece. The neck of the guitar is protected from the pressure of the string by a leather thong attached to the cross-piece. A more modern form of *cejilla* is made of metal with a rubber lining and with a plastic cross-bar and nylon strap. This variety is especially quick to apply and adjust, though uglier than the traditional kind, some of which are very beautifully made.

1.18 Cejilla – *traditional type.*

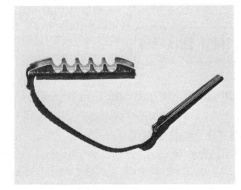

1.19 Cejilla – *Jim Dunlop model.*

All the excerpts of music in this book beyond this page are played on the cassette with the *cejilla* at the fret indicated at the top of the written music. The notation and *cifra* are written as if the *cejilla* was not being used. Open strings are still represented as EBGDAE from 1st to 6th rather than their actual pitch (which, for example, will be F♯ C♯ A E B F♯ if the *cejilla* is at the 2nd fret). Similarly, chord positions for the left hand and individual notes are named in the text according to their positions relative to the *cejilla*, as if it was the nut. This allows open strings, chord positions and fingering to be easily recognised, irrespective of the fret-position at which the *cejilla* is placed.

Tuning with CEJILLA in place
When using the *cejilla* it will be necessary to check the tuning with the *cejilla* fixed in place. Its pressure on the strings limits the direct transmission of changes in tension of the string produced by adjustments of the machine-heads or pegs. When the pitch of the string you are tuning is too low, pulling firmly with a left hand finger on the string between nut and *cejilla* may raise the pitch to the required degree. Conversely, if the string is too high in pitch, firm pressure downwards on the string with the right hand thumb will lower it. Alternatively you can push the string outwards away from the fingerboard with your right thumb in the playing position.

LESSON 2 Part One   Introducing Soleares

The rhythm of Soleares takes you deep into the heart of Flamenco, for it is a *toque* which embodies many of Flamenco's most vital elements of rhythm and harmony and from which many other *toques* are derived. In Andalucía, every student of the flamenco guitar will start with it.

The rhythmic structure *('compás')* of Soleares plays so central a role that when you can truly *dominate* it with the completeness of your feeling for its emphatic pulse, you will already be far on the road to becoming a flamenco guitarist. You have to absorb its powerful momentum into your very bones by playing it over and over again, so many times that your friends and family are driven almost mad with it.

As so often in Flamenco, the exact historical origins of Soleares are uncertain and controversial. Probably the most important centre of its development was the Triana district of Sevilla in the early nineteenth century but other localities, too, have strongly influenced it and given it their own distinctive style. The *Cañas* and *Polos* are often said to be older forms but some flamenco historians have suggested that Soleares is earlier still, possibly derived from less serious *toques* used as dance accompaniments. As it is performed today, whether as guitar solo or in accompaniment to song and dance the *Toque por Soleares* is a solemn and majestic rhythm, rich in passionate sentiment and melancholy grandeur.

The word *'soleá'* is probably a corruption of *soledad* which means solitude or loneliness; *soleares*, the plural form, would be *soledades* in Castillian Spanish. The *coplas* (song-verses) of the *cante* are sometimes ironically philosophical but more usually the themes are of romantic tragedy, desolation and death.

The cassette recording of Soleares

First listen to the Soleares on the cassette called 'First Soleares'. This forms the basis for study in Lessons 2, 3 and 4. The whole solo is first heard at a speed which is correct for Soleares and which you can aim to achieve when you have become thoroughly familiar with the piece. You will next hear it recorded as a series of short sequences played separately at a slow speed, so that you can hear their structure clearly. In the text, each sequence will be discussed in turn and new techniques for the right and left hand will be described as they are introduced in the music.

CASSETTE: FIRST SOLEARES

When you study each sequence, your first aim should be to play it in an absolutely even rhythm, at the kind of slow speed heard on the cassette. It will greatly help you to develop your feeling for the rhythm if you try to play along with the cassette, repeating each sequence again and again until you have really mastered it before going on to study the next.

In Lesson 2 we will study the basic rhythm of Soleares and the first sequence of the music.

The COMPÁS of Soleares

The rhythm of Soleares is based on a repeated pattern of 12 equally spaced beats, with accents on the 3rd, 6th, 8th and 10th beats and with a more variable accent also on the 12th. Each sequence of 12 beats makes up one *compás*.

Try to get the feeling of this *compás* first by counting aloud repeatedly at a steady, even pace the numbers 1 to 12, emphasising the numbers shown below in bold print by saying them more loudly:

1   2   **3**   4   5   **6**   7   **8**   9   **10**   11   **12**

Keep the rhythm regular by beating time with your left foot (keeping the heel on the ground and moving the instep up and down so that you count the beats each time it contacts the floor). Now play back the whole 'First Soleares' recording on the cassette again and try to count this rhythm aloud in time with the music you hear, starting from the count of 'one' on the first beat of the music. The accented numbers will coincide with accented beats heard in the music on the tape. Beats 11 and 12 of the first *compás* are heard as taps on the guitar.

You will now be ready to learn to play the first of the sequences played at a slow speed on the recording:

First Soleares (Introduction: first two compases)

Cejilla at 2nd fret

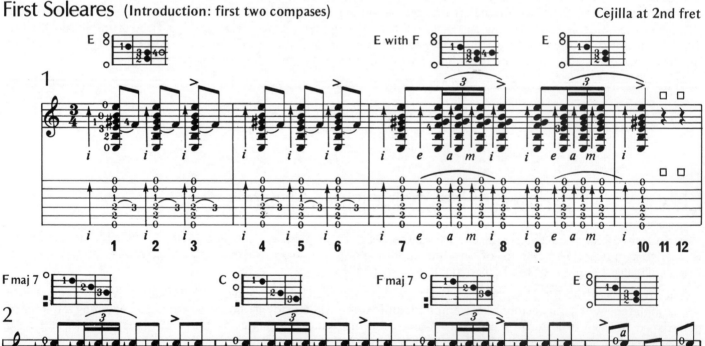

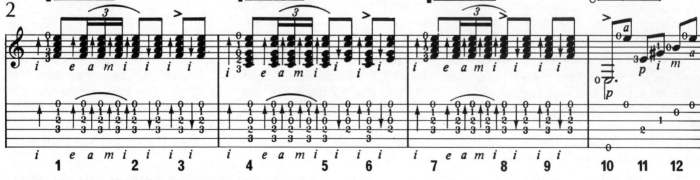

CASSETTE: THE FIRST TWO COMPASES

Note: In the chord diagrams, O opposite a string indicates that it is played open. ■ indicates that the string is not sounded.

16

The first sequence

The first sequence of Soleares consists of two *compases*, each of which has 12 beats in the pattern of the *compás* just described. The first 12-beat *compás* introduces the use of the 4th finger of the left hand and the techniques of *ligado* and *golpe*. These techniques will now be described.

LIGADO 'hammering on'

The first 6 beats are index finger *rasgueo* downstrokes on the chord of E major, using all six strings and resting the thumb on the rosette. Each one is followed by the note F on the intervening half-beats. These latter correspond to the 'ands' when you count aloud 'one-and-two-and-three-and-four-and-five-and-six-and'. These notes derive from the special scale, often called the Phrygian mode because of its similarity to this early ecclesiastical scale, in which Soleares is played. The dissonance they introduce gives a typically flamenco sound.

2.1 E major position for beginning Soleares. Cejilla *shown at second fret.*

The F's are played *ligado* on the 4th string by the technique of 'hammering on'. The term *ligado* (Spanish for 'tied') refers to sequences of notes sounded by the left hand only, without the use of the right hand. The symbol for *ligado* (in both the notation and *cifra*) is ⌒ or ⌣, linking two or more notes of different pitch. Only the first note is sounded by the right hand.

In 'hammering on' a left hand finger descends firmly onto an already vibrating string to sound a note of higher pitch. The F's here are sounded by bringing the tip of your 4th (i.e. little) finger of the left hand down quickly, with a hammer-like action, onto the 4th string to stop it at the third fret, as shown in photos 2.1 and 2.2. It stays down each time for the duration of half a beat. Fingers 1, 2 and 3 hold down the E major chord.

2.2 Little finger has 'hammered' down onto 4th string for the ligado, *sounding an F.*

Two 4-stroke *rasgueos* follow the index downstroke on beat 7. The first of these is played on a chord for which the left hand maintains the E major position but with the little finger again held down to stop the F on the 4th string (i.e. as in 2.2). The little finger is lifted after the index downstroke on beat 9 so that the 4-stroke *rasgueo* leading onto the index downstroke on beat 10 is again on the unembellished E major chord. For these *rasgueos* the thumb rests lightly on the rosette, so that all six strings are sounded.

Correct timing of the 4-stroke *rasgueos* is vital. As described in Lesson 1, the beat of the rhythm coincides with the fourth stroke (with the index), on beat 8 of the *compás* for the first *rasgueo* and on beat 10 for the second.

The GOLPE

The last two beats of the first *compás*, i.e. beats 11 and 12, introduce the technique of *golpe*, indicated by the symbol □ above the beat on which it is played. The *golpe* (Spanish for 'tap') is made by a quick flexion movement of the 3rd finger of the right hand, bringing both nail and flesh into contact with the *golpeador* as shown in photos 2.3 (a) and (b) *[continued overleaf on p.18]*.

2.3 The golpe: *(a) Starting position of third finger.*

(b) Impact. Only the third finger has moved.

The GOLPE (continued)

The movement of the third finger as it plays the *golpe* is from the knuckle, while the rest of the finger and the hand and wrist remain relaxed. Nail and flesh hitting the *golpeador* together give a characteristic sound. After hitting the *golpeador*, the finger stays down in contact with it and is only lifted at the beginning of the next stroke. The movement should not be too forceful.

Later, you will find that the *golpe* is not only played on its own but is also played simultaneously with strokes by thumb or index which sound the strings.

The second *compás* of Soleares brings in two new chords, shown in diagram form with the music. The first, a chord of F major with an open 1st string sounding E is shown in photo 2.4. The chord may be named as F major 7 (F major with added major seventh). The other chord, of C major, is shown in 2.5.

2.4 F maj 7 position.   *2.5 C major position.*

For the *rasgueos* in this *compás*, since the chords do not include notes on the sixth string, the right hand thumb rests lightly on the sixth string to stabilise the hand.

Practise the two *compases* of the first sequence slowly and gently at first, aiming for absolute accuracy of rhythm and emphasis on the accented beats. Beginners will find it hard initially to maintain the steady pulse of the rhythm on moving on from one 12-beat *compás* to the next. You should repeat the two *compases* together again and again until you can play them with the precise regularity of a metronome. Imagine that you are following a dancer who is marking the accents with her heels.

Another word on notation

You will see that the 12-beat *compases* have been written as four bars of 3 beats each. This is a common convention which helps you to see exactly where you are in the music at any moment, but the bar-lines here, as in most other flamenco music, have no other significance. The accents of the rhythm do not regularly fall on the first beat of the bar as would be expected in conventional notation, and really the concept of bars is quite alien to flamenco rhythm. Throughout this book accented beats will be shown by the symbol > over the beat.

The ending phrase

The last three beats (i.e. the final bar) of the second *compás* are a typical and often-used ending phrase in Soleares, which punctuates passages of melody or *rasgueo* rhythm. You will find such punctuating phrases are common in Flamenco and there can be many subtle variations on the basic pattern. The phrase here is in the form of a broken chord *(arpegio)* of E major. Two different ways of sounding the notes with the right hand are given in this solo, each giving its own distinctive character to the music.

The first method described is shown in the music on p.16. The techniques needed are those already introduced in the Malagueña of Lesson 1, with the additional use of the second and third fingers (m and a) of the right hand to pluck the strings. A thumbstroke on the 6th string is followed by the third finger plucking the 1st string. The thumb then plays the 4th string, followed in regular sequence by i, m and a plucking the 3rd, 2nd and 1st strings, respectively. It is important to keep the rhythm regular, with the notes evenly spaced.

Alternative right hand fingerings for ending phrase.

When you have mastered this way of playing the phrase, try the alternative way of playing it with thumb and index without using the second and third fingers. This gives a stronger sound to the final *arpegio*, as might be appropriate after a passage of rhythm such as this or after a melody played with the thumb (as you will find later on in the solo), or when the guitarist is playing for accompaniment. After the thumb strikes the 6th string, the index finger sounds the open 1st string; the thumb then plays 4th, 3rd and 2nd strings with a followed-through stroke and the phrase ends with the index plucking the open 1st string. This illustrates again the use of the thumb in Flamenco to sound the higher strings as well as the basses. It requires good independence of thumb and index movements if 4th, 3rd and 2nd strings are to be played in the even rhythm required.

LESSON 2 Part Two   A Technical Exercise

for the right thumb and the four fingers of the left hand

This exercise (Ex. 6) is a very good way of developing strength and independent control in the right thumb and all four fingers of the left hand. The techniques introduced in it are of such fundamental importance to Flamenco that they are discussed in detail on this and the next 3 pages. The exercise has not been recorded on the cassette.

There are not many purely technical exercises in the book, since the aim has been to relate all techniques as much as possible to the actual music of Flamenco. Those that are now going to be included are meant for continuing daily practice however advanced you are. You should keep coming back to them, because as you progress you will recognise more and more how vital it is to get the basic hand and finger movements right if you are to get a really good sound from the guitar. It is very easy to fall into bad habits of hand-positioning and technique early on which turn out to be hard to unlearn. Sooner or later they become a big obstacle to further progress and a major source of frustration. A little more time spent now on the basic essentials will be very amply rewarded.

The exercise is in the form of a semitone (chromatic) scale, with all notes played *apoyando* (see below) by the thumb. The *cejilla* is not used. You should try to play the notes *slowly and very evenly*. A steady regularity of rhythm is much more important than speed, which can come later. In the text which follows the music, the movements required of each hand are described and illustrated by photographs.

As already said, you will find it a great help to practise in front of a mirror. If you are confused by the reversal of your image in the mirror when you try to follow the photographs, look at the photos in the mirror so that you can compare their mirror-image with your own.

Ex. 6

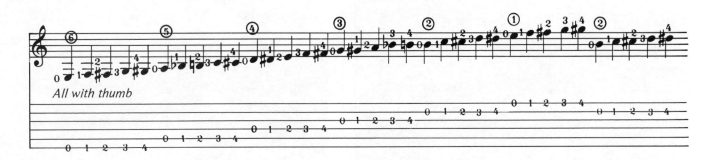

All with thumb

Continue the same pattern from bass to treble, then treble to bass strings, repeatedly.

The right hand

Up until this point, right hand movements have been based on what we can call the 'basic playing position', i.e. with the hand positioned so that the line of the knuckles is nearly parallel to the strings, with the thumb well to the left of the fingers. In this exercise we meet the other main position for the right hand in Flamenco. It is adopted in passages of music played entirely with the thumb, so it will be called the 'thumb' position. The two positions are compared in photos 2.6 to 2.11 overleaf.

BASIC playing position

2.6 *Right hand in the basic position.*

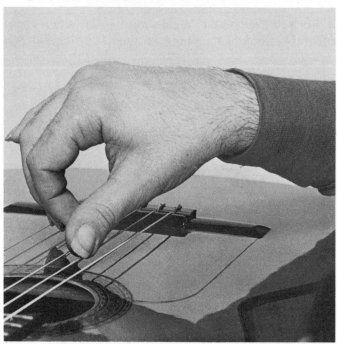

2.8 *Basic position, with plane of back of hand parallel to soundboard.*

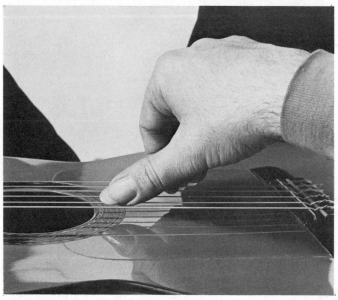

2.10 *Basic position from player's viewpoint.*

THUMB position

2.7 *Right hand in the thumb position.*

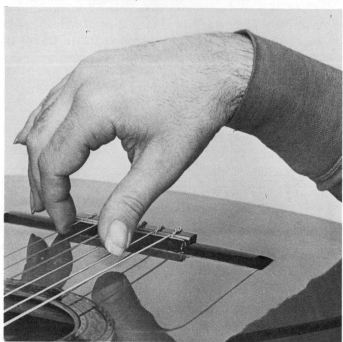

2.9 *Thumb position. Higher arch to wrist.*

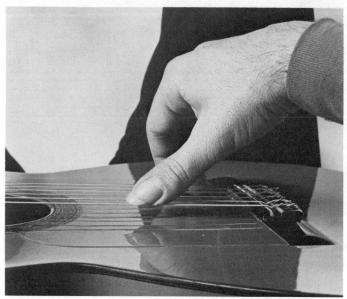

2.11 *Thumb position. Thumb strikes at a steeper angle nearer the bridge.*

The 'thumb' position

You will see from the photographs opposite that for the 'thumb' position the forearm has moved forwards slightly, so that the thumb descends on the strings at a steeper and less acute angle than in the 'basic' playing position. The arch of the wrist is higher, so that the palm of the hand now faces the right shoulder and the line of the knuckles is at more of an angle across the strings. Index and middle fingers, slightly flexed, rest with their tips on the *golpeador* just under the first string and close to the bridge. Ring and little fingers extend forwards to counterbalance the hand. Try to make sure you get a similar 'balanced' look to your hand in the mirror.

The hand is now stabilised and only the thumb moves. The wrist stays very relaxed.

To make each thumbstroke, lift the thumb, then swing it downwards, all the movement coming only from its joint at the wrist. The power of the stroke (and with practice it can become very forceful) simply aids the natural fall of the thumb onto the string through its own weight. The tip of the thumb moves in a line downwards and in towards the front of the guitar. After hitting the string, the thumb continues on until its movement is arrested by silent contact with the next higher string (see photos 2.12 and 2.13). For this reason, the stroke is called *'apoyando'* (Spanish for 'leaning on'). The line of travel of the thumb is towards your third finger. If the movement was continued to its full extent without the strings intervening the tip of the thumb would hit the middle of the 3rd finger.

2.12(a) Position of the thumb as it strikes the 5th string apoyando. Fingers i and m rest on golpeador in contact with 1st string.

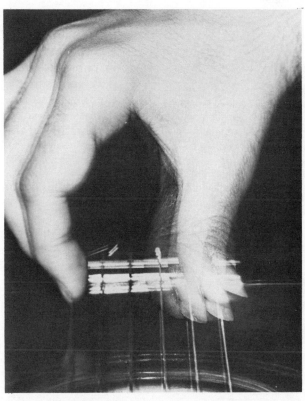

2.13 Multiple exposure to show movement of thumb striking 6th string apoyando. The three superimposed images show the start, impact and end of the stroke.

2.12(b) Thumb at end of stroke, arrested by 4th string.

Callo y uña

The point of impact with the string is on the side of the tip with a combination of flesh and nail *(callo y uña)*. This requires careful shaping of the thumb-nail so that it forms a backing to the flesh, which will soon form a hardening (callus) at this point. The edge of the nail also strikes the string but it should not project so that it catches and limits speed and mobility of the thumb. It is on the thumb that so much of the propulsive power and impetus of Flamenco depends.

Try to get a relaxed 'bouncy' feel to this thumbstroke so that with practice you can play strongly and rapidly.

Different people have very differently shaped thumbs, but the main principles described here apply to all. You do not need a recurved thumb which bends backwards at its middle joint to become skilful with this technique; a straight thumb can do it just as well.

2.14 The left hand. One finger to each of four frets on the 6th string.

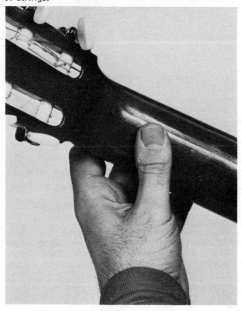

2.15 One finger to a fret on the 1st string. Line of knuckles parallel to fretboard. Fingertips vertical to strings.

2.16 Position of left thumb at back of neck. The fingers are stopping the chord of E major.

The left hand

Exercise 6 is a good basis for learning important principles of left hand action. Points to bear in mind include the following:

* Fingertips vertical to strings

Stop the strings as close to the frets as you can without damping the sound, so that there is no buzz from the fret. Bring your fingers down on the string as nearly as possible at rightangles to the plane of the fingerboard. The pressure of their tips on the strings is balanced by the thumb, without undue tension or any pull by the arm.

* Thumb straight, stationary and opposite fingers

Keep the left hand thumb positioned opposite the fingers and in contact with the neck on or near to a line down the middle of the neck, as shown in photo 2.16. As you ascend from 6th to 1st string, the thumb moves only very slightly round the neck from the middle towards the side of the fingerboard away from you (see 2.17). The thumb does not bend and it does not stick out to the left. Remember the left hand does not support any of the weight of the guitar.

* Finger flexion on changing strings

Since the thumb moves only enough to maintain the tips of the fingers vertical to the fretboard the fingers must bend more at their middle joints as you ascend from 6th to 1st string. Compare photos 2.14 and 2.15.

* Knuckles parallel to strings

Make very sure that the line of the knuckles stays parallel to the edge of the fingerboard. A good way of working on this is to imagine you are trying to keep the palm at the base of the little finger nearer to the edge of the fingerboard than the palm at the base of the 1st finger. You will not actually achieve this but keeping this aim in mind will help you overcome a very common and disabling fault in the left hand. This is to let the fingers come down at an angle to the strings rather than square across them; 3rd and 4th fingers will then have much further to travel to stop the strings and you will not be able to develop the necessary strength, speed or accuracy in their use.

* Relaxed wrist

In any fret-position on the guitar, whether here, in what is called the first position, or later on in higher positions, you need to keep the basic posture of the hand in relation to the fingerboard constant. The wrist must stay relaxed. You will find that the book contains a considerable number of photographs of left hand chord positions or 'shapes' as they are often called. The main purpose of these is to illustrate the basic posture of the hand and fingers.

* One finger per fret

If the knuckles are parallel to the edge of the fingerboard, each finger naturally overlies a different fret-space and in this exercise is brought down in sequence 1 to 4 without the hand as a whole moving. Photo 2.18 shows how each of the fingers descends onto the string.

2.17 *Position of thumb when fingers stop only the 1st string. It has moved slightly nearer the edge of the fingerboard.*

* Economy of movement

It is an important principle of left hand action that there should be a minimum of unnecessary movements of the fingers. Otherwise, facility and speed are hindered and the movements of the fingers will waste effort and look untidy. The fingertips should stay close to the fingerboard, so that they move only a short distance to stop strings. This is shown, for example, in the photographs of left hand chord shapes: you will see that the non-stopping fingers stay poised close to the fingerboard. It can even be difficult to tell from the photographs alone which fingers are actually pressed down onto the strings (hence the need for chord diagrams in addition to the photos).

* Checking the indentations

Because each finger should descend on the strings at a constant point on its tip, you will find the flesh of the tip becomes indented and then forms a hardened callus at a constant point. Notice carefully where the indentations fall and the angles made by the strings on each finger. As a general rule the indentations on the middle finger should lie parallel to the fingerboard.

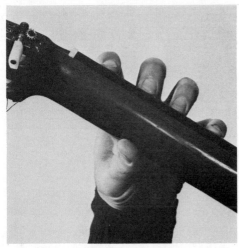

2.18 *Angles of fingers relative to each other as they descend onto 6th string.*

Elements of Flamenco 2   Toques

At the beginning of this lesson Soleares was introduced as an example of a flamenco *toque*. The word *toque* (from the Spanish verb *tocar*: 'to touch' or 'hit' and hence 'to play an instrument') is actually used in three senses. *El Toque* embraces the whole art of flamenco guitar-playing, just as *El Cante* denotes flamenco singing and *El Baile*, flamenco dance. We may also speak of the *toque* of a particular guitarist *(tocaor)* when we refer to his repertoire and style of playing. It is, however, in a third sense that the word is most commonly used here when we refer to the different rhythmic forms of Flamenco as *toques*, of which Soleares is a very important one. Other *toques* of central importance in Flamenco include Seguiriyas, Alegrías, Bulerías, Tangos and Fandangos.

Each *toque*, commonly named in the plural as, for example, Soleares or *toque por* (for) Soleares, is a form or type of Flamenco. There is no exact English equivalent for '*toque*' used in this sense, but as you become more familiar with Flamenco you will soon find that the different *toques* are easily distinguished. Each has a characteristic and recurring pattern of beats and accents (i.e. its *compás*) and it also has its own kinds of key and harmonic structure. As a result it has not only a particular rhythmic form but also a characteristic sound and range of expression. Historically the *toques* have different regional origins, and their name often reflects this. The dance *(baile)* and song-verses *(coplas)* of the styles of singing *(cante)* associated with each toque are also distinct.

Some *toques* do not have a consistently regular rhythm so that they are said to be *en toque libre* ('in free time'). They include many forms of Fandangos and their regional variants. The majority of *toques*, however, have both a regular beat and a very definite pattern of accented beats which together make up the *compás*. As was said earlier, this metrical emphasis is adhered to very strictly by the guitarist both in passages of *rasgueo* and in his *falsetas*.

Two examples of *falsetas* will be introduced in the next lesson.

LESSON 3 Soleares (continued)

The next sequence of Soleares continues with two more 12-beat *compases* of rhythmic *rasgueo*. The second of these is an example of a *llamada*. It is followed by the first *falseta*, a melody played by the thumb.

First listen to this sequence played at a slow speed on the cassette. A description of the techniques used follows the music:

CASSETTE: LESSON 3, RHYTHM COMPÁS, LLAMADA, FIRST FALSETA

Cejilla at 2nd fret

FALSETA 1

Rhythm COMPÁS

The first *compás* of rhythmic *rasgueo* in this lesson (the third *compás* of the complete solo) is similar to the second one in the previous lesson except that the 1st string is now stopped at the third fret by the 4th finger of the left hand (giving the note G) instead of being played open. The new chord shapes are shown in 3.1 and 3.2.

3.1 Position of F maj 7 with G on 1st string instead of E (called F9).

3.2 Position of C major with G on 1st string.

3.3 Position of E7 (with open 4th string).

LLAMADA

The next *compás* of *rasgueo* returns to the harmonic structure of the *compás* at the start of the complete solo (i.e. the first *compás* of Lesson 2). It is of the type called a *llamada* (Spanish for 'call'), an emphatic statement of the *compás* which signals the introduction to the *cante* or *baile* or, as here, a passage of melody. This *llamada* is based on the chords of E major and F major 7, the latter being played on beats 3, 7 and 9. Beat 2 is a chord of E7, so called because it includes the note D on the open 4th string (as shown in photo 3.3).

The 4-note chords on beats 7, 8 9 and 10 are each played with a thumbstroke (p) across the top four strings. This type of thumbstroke is particularly important in Soleares. It is strong and deliberate, the thumb pushing firmly downwards and forwards at an angle across the strings. Each string is sounded with equal force in succession so that the effect is of a rapid *arpegio* (broken chord) rather than a single beat. The right hand is in the 'thumb' position and the wrist remains almost completely stationary, with just a slight rotation as the thumb sweeps across the top four strings. The start and finish of the stroke are shown in 3.4.

3.4 Thumb downstroke across top four strings: (Left) striking the 4th string, (Right) end of stroke.

The last two beats of the *llamada* are silent 'rests'. They must be given their full time-value so that the *falseta* which follows starts on the right beat of the *compás*. It will help you to get the feel of these silent beats if to start with you tap a *golpe* (or your foot) on each of them.

First FALSETA

The first *falseta* for Soleares is a traditional one in which the melodic passages are played *apoyando* with the thumb, with the right hand in the 'thumb' position. This is the technique described in Part Two of Lesson 2.

Like many of the older traditional *falsetas* for Soleares, this one occupies 24 (i.e. 2 x 6 + 12) beats. The first half consists of a melodic phrase of three beats followed by an ending type of *arpegio* over three more, played twice. The accents fall on beats 3 and 4 as shown in the music. The melody is in triplets, with three notes sounded within the duration of one beat.

The accents in the second half of the *falseta* follow the basic Soleares *compás*.

It is just as essential to play *falsetas* with correct accentuation as it is to emphasise them in *rasgueo*. This will give meaning to the melody and keep alive the rhythmic urge of the *compás*.

The *falseta* has 3 ending-phrase *arpegios*. To play these, the right hand remains in the 'thumb' position and the alternative method of striking with thumb and index described on p.18 is used.

25

Second FALSETA

The second *falseta*, recorded separately at a slow speed on the cassette, is another traditional one and you will hear it in many versions. It is based on a sequence of chords (A minor, C major, F maj 7, C, F maj 7, E major). The left hand fingering for these is shown in chord diagrams with the music. The rhythm is the basic 12-beat *compás* of Soleares (repeated once in the solo).

CASSETTE: SECOND FALSETA

FALSETA 2   Cejilla at 2nd Fret

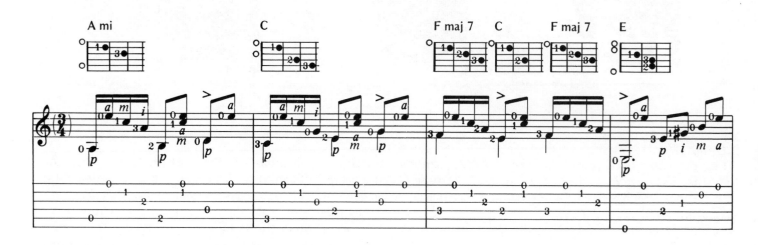

A bass melody is played with *apoyando* strokes of the thumb. Each note of melody is followed by a 3-note *arpegio*, a 2-note chord or a single note on the open 1st string; these fill out the music and form an accompaniment to the melody. The *arpegios* are of the type sometimes called 'back' *arpegios*, since the treble strings are struck in order from higher to lower pitch (**a, m, i** on strings 1, 2, 3 in turn) — in contrast to the 'forward' *arpegio* already mentioned in which the order is the reverse (i.e. **i, m, a** from lower to higher pitch). All the notes played by **a, m** or **i** are played *tirando*, a technique which is described in detail below. First, however, there are two technical points worth noting in the left hand.

Left hand technique

The *falseta* illustrates an important aspect of flamenco guitar playing, in the way the music is created on the basis of a series of chord positions or 'shapes' held down by the left hand. Many *falsetas* are made up in this way. Individual fingers of the left hand move to stop (or unstop) strings to make the melody notes, while other fingers stay down on the strings in their position in the chord shape. In some of the earlier pieces of the music in this book, diagrams and chord symbols are included to show where chord positions are to be held down. With experience, you will recognise from the patterns of notes in the music where it is appropriate for the left hand fingers to adopt and maintain a chord position on several strings at once rather than to stop just one note at a time.

A second important point of technique is illustrated by this *falseta*. When the left hand fingers move from one chord shape to another, you should move only those fingers which take up new positions: any finger which will be stopping the same string at the same fret in the new chord as in the previous one should not be lifted from the fingerboard. You may already have recognised this in the second *compás* of Lesson 1 where there is a chord change from F maj 7 to C and then another back to F maj 7; the first finger remains stationary on the 2nd string while the chord changes are made by movements of the 2nd and 3rd fingers. The first finger again illustrates the point in this *falseta*. It should stay pressed down behind the first fret on the 2nd string from beat 1 right through until immediately before beat 10. The note C which it stops is included in all the chords until beat 10, when the fingers move to take up the chord position of E major for the ending phrase which occupies the final 3 beats.

The TIRANDO stroke

Tirando and *apoyando* are the two main ways of striking individual strings with the right hand fingers or thumb. *Apoyando* has already been described for the thumb: the striking finger or thumb comes to rest against the next adjoining string at the completion of the stroke. In *'tirando'* ('pulling') the line of impact is parallel to the sound-board of the guitar rather than down towards it as in *apoyando*, and the striking finger (or thumb) does not touch an adjacent string.

The hand adopts the 'basic' playing position for *tirando*. In this position the middle finger, as seen from the player's viewpoint, is at rightangles to the strings. Index finger and thumb from this viewpoint cross in an ✗ shape as shown in photo 3.5, when fingers **a, m** and **i,** rest on strings 1, 2 and 3, respectively, with the thumb resting on a bass string, well to the left of the fingers. This important point ensures that thumb and fingers can move independently of each other.

Photo 3.6 shows the movement of a finger striking the string *tirando*. From its starting point a short distance from the string the finger accelerates instantly to strike the string with the tip of the nail and stops after a follow-through which is clear of the adjacent string. The line of travel on impact is parallel to the soundboard.

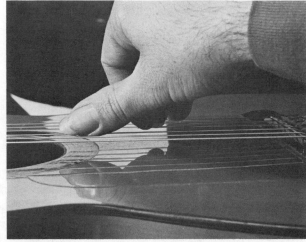

3.5 ✗ *shape formed by fingers and thumb as seen by player. Thumb strikes well to the left of fingers.*

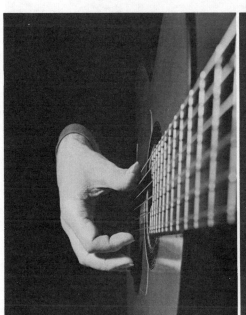

3.6 *Index finger* tirando: *(a) Starting position.*   *(b) Impact. Tip-joint bends backwards.*   *(c) End of stroke.*

3.7 *Movement of the index* tirando *when carried to its full extent so that it touches the base of the thumb (practice exercise only).*

Movement from the knuckle

Try to move the whole finger from its joint at the knuckle. This is essential. The tip of the finger moves in a line directed towards the ball of the thumb, not hooking into the palm of the hand. You will see in photo 3.6 (a) that the middle joint of the finger is bent to almost a rightangle at the start of the stroke. The finger bends slightly more at this joint as the stroke is made, but the main power behind the stroke comes from the swing of the whole finger from the knuckle-joint. To get the correct feeling of the movement of the fingers, practise by playing *very* slowly and by continuing the movement of the finger on after striking the string until the fingertip comes to rest against the ball of the thumb (see 3.7). Normally the finger will not move so far, but the exercise emphasises the way the fingers move primarily from the knuckle-joints. The third finger (*el dedo torpe:* the sluggish finger) will need particular attention in this respect because it is initially weaker than the others.

At the moment of impact the tip-joint of the striking finger will actually bend *backwards* slightly if the finger is fully relaxed (3.6(b)). This, too, is a useful point to achieve when you are trying to concentrate on getting the finger moving from the knuckle. In *tirando* playing the fingers are not so completely relaxed all the time. The exact degree of tension will vary with the context in the music (and also to some extent with the individual player).

27

3.8 Posture of the fingertips in relation to the strings. Each fingernail contacts the string at the apex of the nail, but only the middle fingernail comes square-on to the string. The index finger inclines towards the side nearer the player, the third finger towards the side further away.

3.9 Thumb apoyando with the hand in the 'basic' position. (Top) Before striking the 6th string. (Above) End of stroke, arrested by 5th string.

When playing *arpegios*, as in this *falseta*, each finger moves independently of the others. For chords, where two or more strings are struck simultaneously, the striking fingers move together from the knuckle with the same movement as for a single finger. The angles at which the three fingers descend onto the strings are demonstrated in 3.8.

Only the fingers (and thumb) move in striking the strings: the rest of the hand and the wrist are relaxed and *do not move at all*.

The thumb
In the 'basic' playing position, the thumb, as you will see in photos 3.9, lies more along the line of the strings than it does in the 'thumb' position. In the *falseta* the thumb plays *apoyando*; the impact is more on the side of the tip of the thumb, again with a combination of nail and flesh.

It may be mentioned at this point that in *tirando* playing with the *thumb* the movement is essentially similar, except that the follow-through of the stroke then clears the next higher string rather than coming to rest against it as in *apoyando*. The movement of the tip is thus in a roughly circular or oval path at rightangles to the plane of the strings, with the thumb moving entirely from its joint at the wrist without bending at either of the other two joints. Thumb *tirando* is not very much used in Flamenco.

Movement of the thumb should be completely independent of movements of the fingers. This independence of control is vital for good right hand technique.

More about the basic playing position of the right hand
If the right hand and wrist are correctly relaxed, you should have no difficulty in getting the hand to form the important angle at the wrist with the forearm shown in photo 3.10. The weight of the relaxed hand will be enough to maintain it. This angle ensures that the line of the knuckles is just about parallel to the strings, an important point if the fingers are to strike the strings correctly. To begin with there is a tendency to straighten the wrist rather than making sure the hand is angled downwards and away from you. This error will bring the hand round so that the knuckles are at too much of an angle with the strings.

Another point to note in the right hand is the fairly flat arch to the wrist, which means that the plane of the

28

back of the hand lies roughly parallel to the front-surface of the guitar. Too high an arch will limit the power the fingers can exert. (You can prove this to yourself by seeing what happens when you support your full weight off the ground by hanging by your fingertips; the wrist naturally straightens and even bends backwards if you are to exert the necessary force).

The right hand side of the palm should be brought down fairly close to the front of the guitar and should not be further from it than the left side (as seen when the hand is in the playing position). This is a characteristic feature of the right hand in Flamenco: it brings the 3rd finger strongly onto the strings.

The positioning of the knuckles in relation to the strings serves as a useful reference point in studying the details of right hand technique. The degree to which their line approaches a line parallel to the strings, their distance

3.10 In the 'basic' position the right hand is angled downwards at the wrist, away from the line of the forearm. Photo 1.1 also shows this clearly.

from the strings, which strings they overlie and their normal distance from the bridge — all these points are likely to vary slightly for best results according to the shape of your hands and the kind of tone you want from the guitar. As your technique advances you will be able to explore the effect of altering these to suit best the action of your hand. To start with, however, you would be well advised to copy the photos in these respects as closely and precisely as you can.

The aim of this book is to describe major principles of technique and also to provide a model (by means of the photographs) which will help you lay down a really sound basis for developing musical facility and good tone. These major principles mostly stress the points of similarity you will notice if you watch different professional flamenco players. You will, of course, also notice minor differences between them in the way their hands and fingers move. These small differences result from individual preference and convenience and it would be foolish to attempt any definitive statement as to which is generally superior. What suits one player best may not suit another quite so well.

An exercise for LIGADO

To conclude Lesson 3 we have another technical exercise, this time written in the same rhythm as the first *falseta* played with the thumb. Besides illustrating the techniques already described, it takes the *ligado* technique of 'hammering on' a stage further by using fingers 1, 2 and 3 of the left hand. The *falseta* structure will help you to get the timing right.

In the *ligado* passages, an open string is struck *apoyando* by the thumb and then 1st, 2nd and 3rd fingers are 'hammered on' in sequence to sound a chromatic phrase occupying the duration of one beat.

CASSETTE: LIGADO EXERCISE

Ex.7

Cejilla at 2nd fret

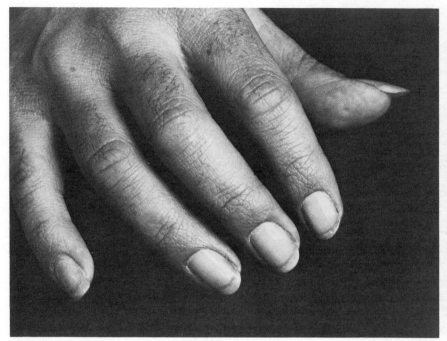

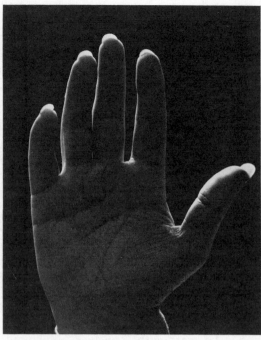

3.11 The right hand fingernails.

3.12 Fingernails of the right hand seen by translucent light with the fingertips at eye level.

Elements of Flamenco 3   Fingernails

Your fingernails of the right hand are going to be very important to you in playing the flamenco guitar. It is the impact of the nail which makes the string vibrate, so each must be long enough to produce a clean, incisively clear note. The nails must not be so long, however, that they hinder the mobility of the fingers.

If the nails are the right length, then in *apoyando* and *tirando* playing the fleshy extremity of the fingertip will just touch the string before the latter is hit by the projecting end of the nail. This light brush with the flesh helps guide the nail onto the string but it makes no significant contribution to the sound. In *rasgueo*, too, the nails are essential in producing the brilliant 'attack' so characteristic of the exciting sound of Flamenco. With the thumb, as already mentioned, sound production is by a combination of nail and flesh.

There are some guitarists who become nail-neurotics: they talk fingernails, think fingernails — perhaps even dream fingernails. But this does not mean that the proper care of your nails has to be a daunting and difficult business. They need careful shaping and strengthening to meet Flamenco's demands on them, but you will find that time devoted to their preparation and protection is amply rewarded by your greater enjoyment and progress. You should soon be able to find a routine that suits you.

Shaping
Shaping of the ends of the right hand nails (and the smoothing of any projecting irregularities on their playing surface) is best done with fine-surfaced emery-boards. The nails can then be further smoothed with the very finest grade of emery paper. Coarser abrasives such as metal files should be avoided. One can give the tips a final polish by

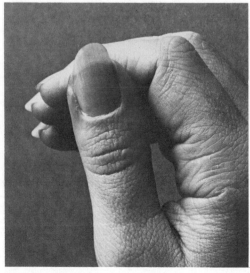

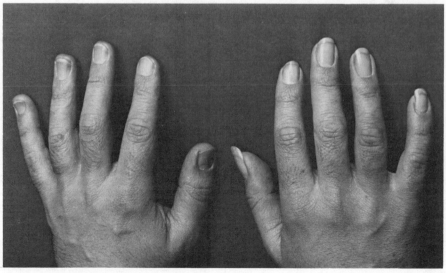

3.13 The right thumbnail.

3.14 Nails of right and left hands compared.

rubbing them against a piece of leather or, to follow a practice among some professionals, against the back (not the sides) of a match-box.

Note the length and shaping of the right hand nails in the photographs. With the palm of the hand facing you and the tips of the fingers level with your eyes, the nails should project about 1/16 inch (1 - 1.5 mm) beyond the fingertips. Hold them up to the light and you will get a good view of the translucent tips of the nails (see photo 3.12). Different players may prefer slightly different lengths of nail but you are strongly advised to start with the relative length illustrated before you consider making any slight modifications to suit your own playing style as it develops.

The little finger-nail can be longer than the others. It is used only for *rasgueos*, where its extra length can partially compensate for the shortness of the little finger compared to the other fingers.

Correct shaping of the right hand thumb-nail (3.13) is critical, particularly on the side where it contacts the string, so that flesh and nail can strike together. People often remark with surprise on the length of the rest of the thumb-nail; this helps the thumb to produce a good sound, particularly in upstrokes as you will later find used in the technique of *alzapúa*.

The fingernails of the left hand are kept smoothly rounded and fairly short (Photo 3.14). They must not be too short, since they are required to give a firm backing to the flesh: this will allow you to produce a strong sound in *ligado* 'pulling-off' (see Lesson 5).

Protection and strengthening

Even the thickest fingernails will need some protection if they are not to be abraded and damaged by impact with the strings. If your nails are thin, they will need additional support and strengthening for good tone-production.

Several methods are used. A good method is first to apply a base-coat of a clear nail-lacquer, Cutex 'Strongnail'. Once this is dry, one or more thin coats of cellulose glue can be applied evenly over it and can be built up in layers to the required thickness. In Spain, 'Pegamento Imedio' is the flamencos' favourite. In the U.K. 'Durafix' by Rawlplug has fairly similar properties. The glue should not be applied directly to the nail but only to the base-coat of Cutex. It is best spread thinly and evenly to prevent bubbles forming as it dries. Place a small blob from the tube onto the surface of the lacquered nail and quickly spread it out with a finger of the left hand, using a different (and corresponding) left hand finger for each nail so that you have a clean fingertip for smoothing the glue on each right hand nail. Some players like to provide added strength by applying the glue together with one or more layers of thin tissue, 'Micropore' adhesive tape or teased out cottonwool, but glue alone is usually adequate.

To prevent the nails drying out from these applications it is advisable to remove the protection every day. Sometimes it peels off easily. Otherwise, use nail-polish remover which contains added oil.

All sorts of things, to be applied or consumed, have been advocated at one time or another as indispensable for strong nails, but many seem based more on superstition than science. Eating gelatin every day (most easily in the form of jelly-cubes) really does seem to help.

Various commercial preparations claim to strengthen nails. 'Tuff Nail' can be helpful if used sparingly as a moisturiser. One should be careful of preparations containing formic acid since they seem capable of softening the nails unduly if used for long. An occasional application of Mavala may help harden the nail and may reduce the risk of flaking and splitting.

Precautions

You will soon develop a heightened awareness of the many hazards to nails you are likely to meet in everyday life and will learn to take the necessary avoiding action. Handles, switches and clock-winders are just a few of them.

It is vitally important not to expose nails to the drying action of detergents and soaps. Washing-up is out of the question. Even the use of rubber gloves can cause trouble.

Carry an emery-board with you at all times to provide first-aid and to prevent small cracks becoming bigger. Larger cracks, tears or flaking may require careful repairs with glue and possibly paper. New cyanoacrylate adhesives which 'bond instantly to skin tissue' (as the makers warn) may perhaps be useful in emergencies if used with proper caution.

Don't blame your nails!

Students of Flamenco often worry about the shape or strength of their nails and feel they are going to present an insuperable obstacle to playing in a really flamenco way. This is always an unnecessary fear.

Experience has shown again and again that a little care and attention will ensure that the nails can be brought to a satisfactory condition. Niño Ricardo had nails, as he said, *'como papeles'* (as thin as paper) yet, with the help of Pegamento, he could produce an incomparably strong sound from the guitar.

LESSON 4 Part One   Soleares (concluded)

The third FALSETA

The following *falseta* is another *arpegio* one, this time based on the right hand fingering **p i m i** on the top three strings. The thumb now plays *tirando*, as well as the fingers, and the right hand is kept in the 'basic' playing position. The left hand chord position on which the *falseta* is based is shown in 4.1.

The *falseta* is made up of three 12-beat *compases*. In the second of these the chord shape made by index and middle fingers of the left hand in the chord of A minor is moved up the fingerboard to the third and sixth positions, indicated in the notation by the Roman numerals III and VI. Positions on the fretboard are numbered according to the fret-space stopped by the index finger of the left hand.

The two fingers are quickly slid along the strings to their new positions without being lifted from the strings. The movement must be so rapid that there is no delay in the *compás;* it must not be made too soon, otherwise the notes of the preceding chord will not be given their proper clarity and duration.

In this chord-changing movement with the left hand, you must keep constant the posture of the left hand in relation to the fingerboard. The left thumb remains in contact with the neck of the guitar and opposite the fingers as the hand moves.

4.1 A minor position on top three strings only.

▭ **CASSETTE: THIRD FALSETA**

Cejilla at 2nd fret

FALSETA 3

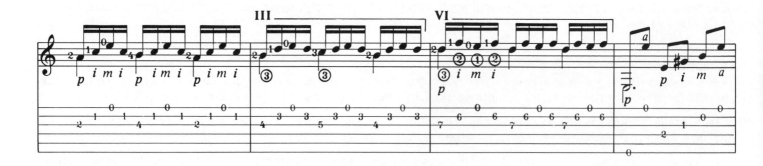

32

Concluding RASGUEO

The Soleares ends with three further *compases* of *rasgueo*. The first two are built on the F C F E sequence of chords as before, but in each there is now the addition of the note D on the second string for the 4-stroke *rasgueo* leading onto beat 8, then F on the first string on beat 9. These new chord shapes are shown in 4.2 and 4.3 and in the chord diagrams below.

The final *compás* returns to the E F E F E chord sequence of the *llamada*. There is a *golpe* on beat 4 followed by an upstroke on the E chord before the downstroke on beat 5, and this needs accurate timing.

4.2 D minor position with E on open 1st string.

4.3 D minor with F's on 1st and 3rd strings.

You will see that the final chord of the solo is played on beat 10. Soleares end on this beat of the *compás*. Beats 11 and 12 are played when another 12-beat *compás* follows on, but are not sounded in the last *compás*.

> 🔲 **CASSETTE : SOLEARES ENDING, THREE COMPASES OF RHYTHM**

First Soleares (final three compases)

Cejilla at 2nd fret

LESSON 4 Part Two   The Technique of Picado

In *picado* (literally 'picked') playing, passages of single notes are played with *apoyando* strokes of alternating right hand fingers. The commonest method is to use alternate strokes with the index and middle finger. With practice the technique can be developed to achieve brilliant speed and attack in playing runs of single notes, but it is also used for slower passages of melody. In Flamenco, single melody notes are always played *apoyando* rather than *tirando*. Sometimes passages of *picado* on higher strings are played with an accompaniment of bass notes played with the thumb *tirando*.

In the following exercise repeated notes are played *picado* on each open string in turn from 1st to 6th and back again to 1st, repeatedly. It provides an excellent basis for a good understanding of the movements involved. A detailed discussion of the technique follows the music. The exercise has not been recorded on the cassette.

Ex. 8

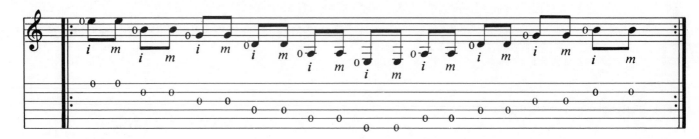

Right hand position for PICADO
The hand position is the same 'basic' position already described for *tirando*, except that the knuckles may lie slightly more over the bass strings as shown in 4.4(a). The knuckles are parallel to the strings and the back of the hand is roughly parallel to the plane of the front of the guitar. The wrist remains relaxed and there is no movement at the wrist joint.

The thumb
The thumb rests lightly on the 6th string to stabilise the hand while notes are played on any of the three treble strings. In a descending run it moves onto the *golpeador* on the near side of the strings when notes are played on the 4th string or on lower bass strings. It moves back again to the 6th string when an ascending run passes from 4th to 3rd and higher treble strings.

The finger movements
In fairly slow passages of *picado* (and you should start by playing the exercise extremely slowly and evenly) the fingers are relaxed. The power of the stroke can be thought of as coming entirely from movement at the knuckles, the two other joints of the finger being somewhat flexed. The alternating movement is as if you were 'walking' the fingers, each taking a swing of equal extent and striking with equal force. Each finger begins its stroke from a short distance (perhaps half an inch or less) from the string. The finger swings in a direction across the strings and also towards the soundboard (i.e. in towards your chest). The tip of the nail hits the string firmly and cleanly and the finger follows through until its tip is brought to rest against the adjacent lower-pitched string. As the nail hits the string the tip-joint is bent backwards by the impact.

When *picado* is played faster or with greater emphasis, the fingers are more rigid and straighter, the movement still coming from the knuckle. Because of the greater rigidity of the fingers, however, the tip-joint does not bend backwards at the moment of impact. For extremely short bursts at maximum speed (which is not appropriate in this exercise) the alternation of the fingers becomes a kind of nervous movement, as one feels for instance if one drums the tips of the straightened fingers as fast as possible on a table top.

Ring and little fingers stay relaxed or the little finger may be extended as shown in photo 4.5. The ring finger will normally move in sympathy with the middle (because of the way the extensor tendons of the fingers are attached).

Practising the exercise
Play the exercise first with alternating index Tand middle fingers, **i-m,i-m**. Then repeat it **m-i,m-i**. Next play it with the alternation of index and third finger, **i-a,i-a** and **a-i,a-i**. Hardest of all, but valuable for the development of the weak third finger, is the alternation **m-a,m-a**, then **a-m,a-m**. Movement of the ring finger should be exactly the same as for the other fingers from the knuckle. The hand should be able to change from one pattern to another without moving as a whole.

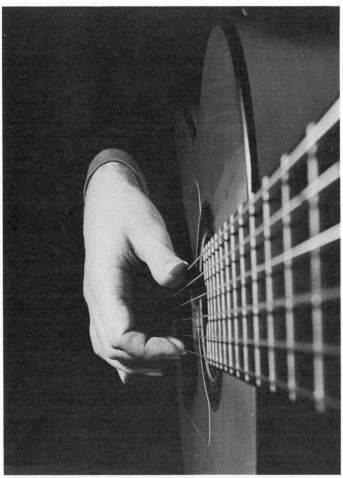

4.4 Picado *with alternate* i *and* m *on the 1st string.*
(a) Index ready to strike 1st string.

(b) Impact of index (shown here with no bending back of the tip-joint).

(c) After striking 1st string index comes to rest against the 2nd

(d) Middle finger arrested by 2nd string after its stroke. Index ready to strike again.

35

4.5 Right hand position for picado *on 1st string. Thumb resting on 6th string; hand in basic position.*

4.6 Picado *on 6th string. Posture of hand essentially unchanged, but arm has bent to bring hand into position. Thumb now rests on guitar.*

PICADO with change of string

As one moves from treble to bass strings or bass to treble, the whole hand moves across the strings (as shown in photos 4.5 and 4.6) in a straight line parallel to the bridge. This maintains the constancy, relative to the strings, of the posture of hand and wrist. In order to keep the point of impact a constant distance from the bridge the elbow is flexed as you move from treble to bass strings and is at the same time drawn outwards and backwards by movement of the upper arm at the shoulder.

Three basic rules of PICADO

can now be stated:

1. The fingers must *always* play alternately, no matter what changes of string occur. Two consecutive notes are never played by the same finger.

2. The fingers move from the knuckle joints, the fingers being alternated strongly and evenly with a swinging action economical in its range of movement.

3. The posture of the right hand and wrist in relation to whichever string is being played by the fingers is kept constant. To maintain this constant posture while changing from higher to lower strings (or lower to higher) the hand is moved in a straight line parallel to the bridge.

The next development of this important exercise is to play it in triplets (i.e. with three notes to each beat). The alternation of the fingers continues unchanged and is independent of the changes of string. You must not pull a finger across from one string to strike the next string. If you do, the rhythm will be made uneven and you will never play good *picado*. Again, practise with the different alternating pairs of fingers, **i-m,i-m; m-i,m-i; i-a,i-a; a-i,a-i; m-a,m-a; a-m,a-m.**

Ex. 9

You can also play it in fours:

Ex. 10

or in single notes as below:

Ex. 11

Another exercise for PICADO

Here is an exercise for *picado* in the form of a simple *falseta* for Soleares. Make sure that the alternation of the fingers is maintained throughout and that each pair of notes starts with the index finger striking the lower-pitched of the two.

▭ CASSETTE: PICADO EXERCISE

Ex.12

Cejilla at 2nd fret

Elements of Flamenco 4   Aire

Aire (literally 'air' and hence 'atmosphere' or 'demeanour') is another word which you will hear often whenever Flamenco is talked about. It means the qualities of animation and expressiveness of a flamenco performance, as determined not only by the form and tempo of the *toque* but also by the personal idiom and style of the performer. In this way even the same piece of music played by different guitarists can communicate very different kinds of *aire*.

In its most general sense *aire* is that special magic which gives Flamenco its essential 'Flamenco-ness'. Strict adherence to the *compás* is a vital part of it, but there is more besides, a quality of meaning which makes the music say something to move the emotions or, at its most intense, to send a shiver down the spine.

The feeling is profound and often tragic in those serious *toques* which comprise the *Cante Jondo* or *Cante Grande* (Deep Song, Great Song). The guitar may then be said to 'lament' *(llorar)* or to produce 'dark sorrows' (*ducas negras* in the gypsy language of *Calé*) if the feeling is especially intense. In the less serious, but often no less intense, *Cante Chico* (Little Song), by contrast, the feeling is more likely to be gay and euphoric, the surge of the music more extrovert and carefree. It is not just the form of the *toque* which decides whether it is regarded as *Jondo* or *Chico*. For some *toques* the distinction is clear: Seguiriyas, for example, are definitely *Jondo*. But for many it depends on the spirit and expressiveness with which it is performed. Malagueñas, for example, can be movingly *Jondo* or lighter and more *Chico* in style.

The gypsy *(gitano) aire* tends to be dissonantly oriental in sound, full of irony and passion and perhaps *cortado* ('cut') by abrupt starts and stops and sudden impulsive accelerations within the overall steady beat of the *compás*. The *aire* of the *Cante Andaluz*, which derives from originally non-flamenco folk-songs of Andalucía, is more open, light-hearted and flowingly melodic. But such distinctions are not always clear-cut and there may still be disputes about how much is *gitano*, how much *Andaluz* in any particular *toque*.

The personal AIRE
At its most personal and idiomatic, *aire* is that characteristic essence which makes the playing of each of the great masters of Flamenco instantly recognisable and unique. The *aire* of a player of the stature of the late Niño Ricardo is an extraordinary, almost tangible aura or 'presence' that is indefinable yet unmistakable.

4.7 Aire *personified. The great gypsy* cantaor, *Rafael Romero, sings* Rondeñas canasteras.

Creating a flamenco AIRE

A feeling for the different kinds of *aire* in Flamenco and the ability to express them on the guitar are facilities which grow the more you absorb yourself in the world of Flamenco through recordings and live performances of every kind. You need a deep commitment and the nurturing of a profound *'afición'* (love) for the flamenco arts and especially for that great mainstream of inspiration, the *Cante*.

It is all too easy to be misled by the virtuosity of the concert guitarist into believing that Flamenco requires prodigious technique and torrents of notes at lightning speed to sound exciting. But this is a profound mistake and one that has led many promising players astray in a search for greater and greater technical brilliance, nearly always at the expense of musicality. There is no musical point at all in playing many notes rapidly where a few with feeling can express more meaning.

If you devote your efforts to laying down a steady, throbbing pulse of the *compás* and making sure, by your phrasing and accentuation, that the music says something with meaning, then you can play true Flamenco right from the start. It will have to be slow in speed at first but you will really be playing Flamenco, not just imitating it.

LESSON 5   Seguiriyas

Seguiriyas are the most profound and passionate of all flamenco *toques*. Like the Soleares, their origins are particularly associated with the *gitanos* of Andalucía. First widely performed in the latter half of the nineteenth century and developed into many individual styles, the Seguiriyas probably derives from song-forms like the *Tonás* which were originally played without guitar accompaniment. A dance version has been devised for theatrical performance, but essentially Seguiriyas belong to the *Cante,* and are an expression of all the most desolate and anguished emotion of the *Cante Jondo.* In the *Cante por Seguiriyas* there is the cry of a man alone with his struggle against misfortune and mortality. Probably nothing in all the folk-music of Europe expresses more poignantly the afflictions of the human soul.

The guitarist who plays Seguiriyas will be inspired by this same tragic intensity of feeling. The performance of Seguiriyas is always something serious and of momentous importance, an event to be countenanced only when the proper atmosphere of *afición* has been created so that the singer can give his all to the *Cante.* If the mood is right, then Seguiriyas can be the occasion for the most intense emotion in Flamenco, when the guitar can indeed become the *guitarra mal herida por cinco espadas* ('guitar mortally wounded by five swords') of Lorca's poem.

The word 'Seguiriyas' is presumed to be a *gitano* version of *Seguidillas,* the name of a popular Spanish dance. The latter is derived from the verb *'seguir'* (to follow) and the term Seguidilla may have been applied loosely to any sequence of verses. There is no other connection between the flamenco *toque* and the Castillian Seguidillas and the names should not be used interchangeably.

The COMPÁS of Seguiriyas

The *compás* of Seguiriyas on the guitar follows a simple and strongly emphasised pattern which is repeated unvaryingly. The way to count it can be shown as follows:

> $\overset{>}{1}$ and $\overset{>}{2}$ and $\overset{>}{3}$ and a $\overset{>}{4}$ and a $\overset{>}{5}$ and

The duration of each of the 12 syllables should be the same, with the accents of the rhythm falling on the numbers. The pattern is repeated again and again.

Play through the cassette recording of the first solo Seguiriyas so that you can start to get the feeling of this powerful rhythm. Count the *compás* aloud as shown above and beat time to the music with your foot, if you can, bringing your foot down to coincide with each of the numbered beats.

 **CASSETTE: LESSON 5, SEGUIRIYAS**

It is conventional to represent the *compás* of Seguiriyas in musical notation in alternating bars of 3/4 and 6/8 time. In the notation below you will see that the *compás* starts on the second beat of a bar in 3/4 time and ends on the first beat of the next bar of 3/4 time.

At first sight this may look complicated, but the complexity lies less in the rhythm than in the way it has to be written in notation. Each note above lasts the same length of time.

There are many passages in Seguiriyas where it may be more appropriate to count the same *compás* slightly differently as:

> 1   2   3   and   4   and   5

Here the duration of each number is twice as long as the time taken up in saying the 'and's.

Combining the two methods and showing the basic *compás* repeated once we have:

Chords for Seguiriyas

Seguiriyas is played on the guitar in the key position called by flamencos *'por medio'*. The starting chord is in the position of A major and the scale, as in Soleares, is in the Phrygian mode. The left hand position for the A major chord is shown in photo 5.1.

Note the way the first finger stops two strings, the third and fourth. If your previous experience with the guitar has made you accustomed to playing this chord with fingers 1, 2 and 3, you should gradually try to make the change-over to the flamenco way described here. This is essential if your 3rd finger is to be free in order to stop other frets during passages where the A major chord is held down (for example the *ligado* 'hammer on' to B flat at the start of the solo, shown in 5.2).

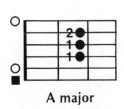

A major

5.1 Chord position of A major.

5.2 *3rd finger 'hammers on' for the ligado.*

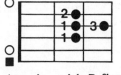

A major with B flat

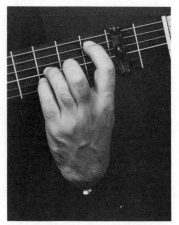

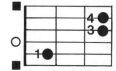 5.3 *B flat chord for Seguiriyas.*

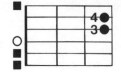 5.4 *Starting chord for* **Falseta 1.**

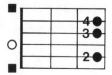 5.5 *Next, C stopped on 5th string.*

The other chord most used in Seguiriyas is a version of B flat major which is shown in 5.3 and in the chord diagram under the photo. Many passages in Seguiriyas are based on this chord. Fingers 3 and 4 hold down their positions while melody notes are played on the 4th and 5th strings using 1st and 2nd fingers together with *ligado* techniques of 'hammering-on' and 'pulling off'.

Two more chords derived from B♭ which occur in the solo and which precede the previous chord in sequence to create a characteristic cadence of Seguiriyas are shown in 5.4 and 5.5 and in the chord diagrams beneath.

LIGADO 'pulling off'

This technique is a second way of sounding notes using only the left hand. We have already met 'hammering on' which produces a higher note than the note first sounded by the right hand. 'Pulling off' produces a lower note. A left hand finger stopping the string plucks it by pulling firmly in a direction across it towards the palm and downwards towards the fingerboard.

In the simplest example the second note is that of an open string: e.g. the notation *(left)* indicates that the middle finger of the left hand stops the 4th string at the 2nd fret; the first note, E, is sounded by the right hand and the second by pulling off with the left middle finger to sound the note, D, of the open string. The symbol for the *ligado* is again a tie, ⌢ or ⌣ .

In other instances the note sounded by 'pulling off' may be stopped by another finger of the left hand, which may then itself be 'pulled off' to sound another, lower note.

An example of two consecutive notes being sounded by 'pulling off', as occurs in the solo to follow, is shown in the notation on the right. The F stopped by the third finger at the 3rd fret on the 4th string is first sounded by the right thumb, with the second finger of the left hand already placed in position to stop the string at the 2nd fret. The third finger pulls off to sound the E and then the second finger pulls off to sound the open string, D. Three notes have been played in sequence but only the first has been sounded by the right hand.

When more than one 'pulling off' occurs consecutively like this, the pulling finger and the stopping finger(s) must be in place at the start when the right hand first plucks the string. A clear note depends not only on the correct movement of the pulling finger but equally on the stopping finger which must brace the string firmly. In the example above, for instance, fingers 3 and 2 must start down together on the frets. This is shown in photos 5.6(a), (b) and (c).

Sometimes the finger which hammers on then sounds the starting note again by pulling off, as in the following example from the solo *(right)*. *Ligado* passages using both hammering on and pulling off to sound a consecutive series of notes are very widely used in Flamenco. It is very important to keep the rhythm of each sequence of notes even and regular otherwise a whole *falseta* could be put out of *compás*.

5.6 Ligado 'pulling off' (a) Starting position with both 2nd and 3rd fingers stopping 4th string.

(b) 3rd finger has 'pulled off' to sound the E stopped by 2nd finger.

(c) 2nd finger has 'pulled off' to sound D of open 4th string.

The solo

The following Seguiriyas consists of a typical introductory passage of *rasgueo* which progresses on to four traditional *falsetas* linked by brief passages of rhythm. A commonly recurring phrase, frequently used to punctuate *falsetas* (or the *cante*) or to act as a 'fill-in' which maintains the rhythm, is the following *compás*:

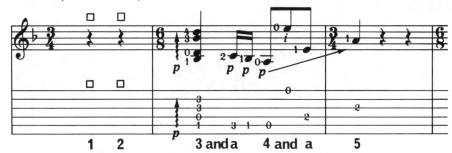

Fingers 3 and 4 stay down from the count of 3 to the count of 4, when the fingers move to the position of the A chord. Note that the C on the 5th string at the third fret is stopped by the 2nd finger. Sometimes an A at the second fret on the 3rd string is played in place of the E on the open 1st string.

The right thumb plays a particularly important part in Seguiriyas. Except for the *rasgueos*, the right hand is in the 'thumb' position throughout.

Note particularly near the end of *Falseta* 2 how the thumb strikes down across two strings (4 and 3, then 5 and 4) together to sound the same note on each (first G then D).

In *Falseta* 3 there is a characteristic type of *arpegio* played on three strings at a time with just thumb and index. The first two notes of each group of four are played in a single followed-through movement with the thumb, striking the lower then the higher string in perfect rhythm.

CASSETTE REPEAT: SEGUIRIYAS

SEGUIRIYAS

Cejilla at 2nd fret

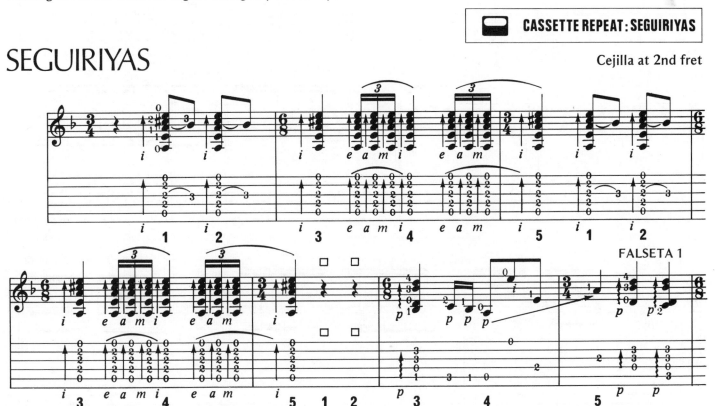

FALSETA 2

FALSETA 3

42

Elements of Flamenco 5   Duende

Duende, literally meaning goblin or elf, is the spirit which inspires those extraordinary, perhaps fleeting, moments in Flamenco (as in other arts like the *corrida*, or bull-fighting) when the performer achieves a total communion with his audience. Only the truest artistry and *afición*, free of any taint of egoism or showmanship, can create the possibility of its occurring. It is an experience of bare truth, when one is somehow transported to the very depth of things, to emotion at its most naked and most poignant, so that one can only feel 'that is how it really is'. An audience of *aficionados* will recognise the experience of *duende* when it comes but it is quickly and unobtrusively passed by. The shiver of recognition is acknowledged, if at all, by perhaps a quiet, almost incredulous murmur of 'olé' before the music sweeps on beyond this brief moment when something touched the soul. It is a rare thing, hardly to be talked about.

LESSON 6 Alegrías

Alegría means 'joy' or 'gaiety' and the Alegrías are a joyful *toque*, light and carefree in spirit. They can express great intensity of feeling, tinged at times with melancholy, but the mood is mostly optimistic and high-spirited in contrast to the agonised, tragic yearning of the previous *toque*, Seguiriyas. You should try to express this optimism and happiness in your playing.

Alegrías belong to the larger family of *toques* called Cantiñas. They originated from the sea-port of Cádiz and probably came into being by the flamenco adaptation of the lively Jotas sung by sailors from Aragon. The melodies of the Jotas were put to the *compás* of Soleares and used for festive dances. Unlike Soleares and Seguiriyas, which are in the Phrygian mode, Alegrías are in the major (and sometimes minor) key, a difference which contributes to their happier and more obviously tuneful *aire*. The *baile por Alegrías* is one of Flamenco's most complex and difficult. The *toque* is danced, sung and played on the guitar.

The COMPÁS of Alegrías
The *compás* of Alegrías is based on a 12-beat pattern identical to that of Soleares, with accents on beats 3, 6, 8, 10, 12. We may, therefore, write it as:

$$1 \quad 2 \quad \overset{>}{3} \quad 4 \quad 5 \quad \overset{>}{6} \quad 7 \quad \overset{>}{8} \quad 9 \quad \overset{>}{10} \quad 11 \quad \overset{>}{12}$$

Counter-rhythms *(contratiempo)* with complex syncopation are common in modern versions.

The solo
The Alegrías in the keys of A major and A minor given here follows a traditional form. After an introduction of *rasgueo* there are three traditional *falsetas* and a *rasgueo* finale. First play the cassette recording of the complete solo while you try to follow the rhythm of it in the written music or *cifra*. The solo has been written down as four sequences of music, so that the techniques required in each sequence can be described and studied in turn as they are introduced. The sequences follow on without a break to make up the solo you will hear on the cassette.

■ CASSETTE: LESSON 6, ALEGRÍAS

Cejilla at 3rd fret

Sequence 1: introduction

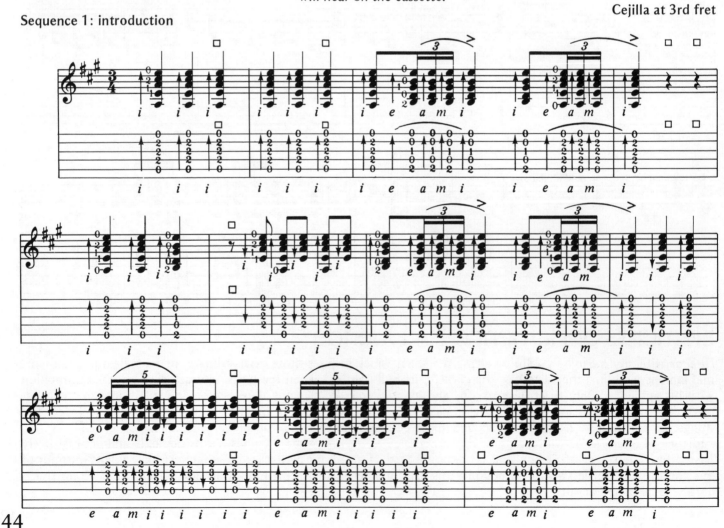

Sequence 1 *(continued)*

We will begin by studying just the first two of the three 12-beat *compases* in this first sequence. The music starts with the chord of A major on the first seven beats. The left hand position for this chord was shown in photo 5.1 and its chord diagram is shown below. A 4-stroke *rasgueo* leads on to beat 8 and this is played on the chord of E7 (the dominant seventh in the key of A major). The left hand fingering was shown in 3.3 and its chord diagram is also shown here *(right)*.

The right hand is in the 'basic' playing position and the thumb rests lightly on the 6th string. The *rasgueos* in the first two *compases* are similar to those you met before in Soleares, but it will be a good idea now to try to learn to combine *golpes* with index downstrokes where these are indicated in the music.

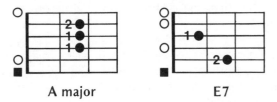

A major   E7

In these first two *compases* and elsewhere in the solo you will see that the square symbol for *golpes* is written over certain accented beats played with index downstrokes. Here they occur on beats 3 and 6. The movement of the 3rd finger of the right hand previously described for the *golpe* is performed at the same moment as the index finger makes a downstroke in its usual way. The impact of the downstroke on the strings and the impact of the 3rd finger on the *golpeador* must both coincide exactly with the beat. There should be no movement of the rest of the hand and the wrist stays relaxed. The movements of the two fingers are independent but simultaneous.

The next *compás* of *rasgueo* (the third in this sequence) introduces a new chord, D major (the subdominant in the key of A). This uses only the top four strings. There is also a new *rasgueo* technique for the right hand in this *compás*.

The chord of D major is shown in photo 6.1.

The 5-stroke RASGUEO

We will call the new *rasgueo* the *5-stroke rasgueo* since 5 strokes are made by the right-hand fingers within the duration of a single beat. There are two differences from the 4-stroke *rasgueo*.

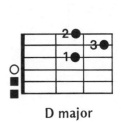

D major

6.1 D major chord position

The first is that the accent of the *rasgueo* falls here on the *first* stroke made by the little finger, and this coincides with the beat of the music. The second is that the *rasgueo* ends with an index finger upstroke after the **e a m i** sequence of downstrokes. In notation, therefore, the *rasgueo* is written as a quintuplet (5 notes to a beat). Later on, in other *toques*, we will meet occasions where the accent coincides with the 5th stroke, the index upstroke, but this is not the case here.

Start by playing the strokes slowly and evenly, emphasising the accent at the beginning of the *rasgueo*. Contrast this with the 4-stroke *rasgueo* where the accent falls on the fourth stroke, made by the index, with the **e a m** strokes preceding the beat.

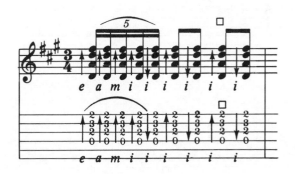

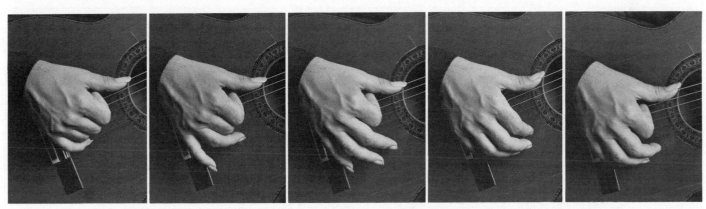

6.2 The 5-stroke rasgueo *shown in sequence with four downstrokes by* e, a, m, i *in turn followed by an index upstroke.*

45

Sequence 2: first FALSETA and rhythm COMPÁS

The *falseta* is played mainly with thumb and index in triplets and is based on the chords of E7 and A major. Note that the *compás* is again the 12-beat pattern with accents on beats 3, 6, 8, 10 and 12. The first *falseta* is followed by another *rasgueo compás* based on the chords D, A, E7, A, with 5-stroke *rasgueos* played on the chords of D and A. On beat 9 in this *compás* we meet another version of the chord of E7, this time played on just the bottom four strings. The fingering is shown in 6.3 alongside the chord diagram.

This beat and the final chord of A major in this *compás* are both played by downstrokes of the thumb at the same time as *golpes* are played with the third finger. As was described earlier for the index downstroke combined with *golpe*, the movements of thumb and third finger must be independent but exactly simultaneous.

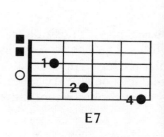

E7

6.3 E7 on lower four strings.

FALSETA 1

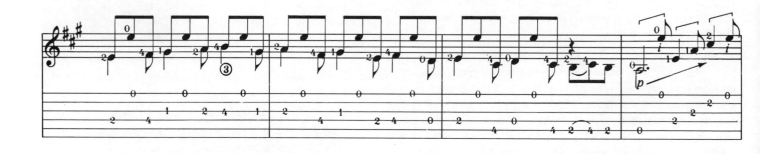

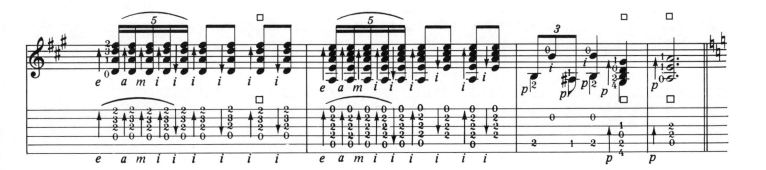

Sequence 3: second FALSETA (CAMPANAS)

This begins with an example of *Campanas* ('bells'). Five chords of A minor and then five of E7 imitate the solemn ringing of a bell and introduce a slow passage played in a minor key (here A minor) with emphatic rhythm. It derives from the form of the *baile por Alegrías.* The *Campanas* follow a climax in the dance which the dancer completes by striking a pose. There is a brief pause and he (or she) begins slowly to move into the rhythm of the dance again before the rhythm starts to build up progressively to a faster pulse, with an extended passage of *zapateado* (footwork) before the finale. Sometimes you may hear the *Campanas* sequence referred to as a *silencio*, but this is not strictly correct. Properly speaking a *silencio* is literally that, a 'silence', when the guitar is silent and the dancer builds up a gradually accelerating *zapateado.*

The slow chords (five chords followed by a *golpe* on the 6th beat of each half of the *compás*) of A minor and E7 in the *Campanas* are played with downward sweeps of the thumb. We have already met the A minor chord in Lesson 1. The melody passages are played *picado* with alternating **i** and **m**, except for the punctuating *arpegios*.

FALSETA 2

47

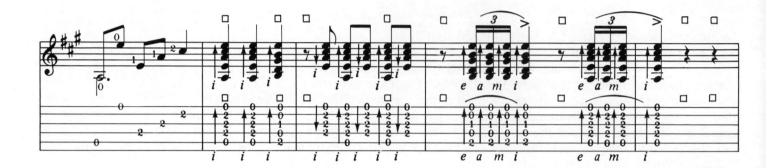

Sequence 3 (above)

In the third bar of the music above, at the point indicated, the left hand fingers take up the position of D minor and hold down the chord for three beats. The chord shape is shown in photo 6.4 and the chord diagram beside it.

Note the six following beats played in octaves. The thumb plays *apoyando*, the index *tirando*. You will find similar octave passages often occurring in Flamenco and it is important to adopt the correct technique of playing them. The emphatic *apoyando* stroke with the thumb sounds the lower of the two notes very slightly before the higher note, sounded by the index. You will hear this clearly on the cassette.

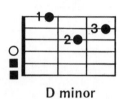

D minor

The D note on the 2nd string can be stopped by fingers 3 or 4, according to context.

6.4 D minor chord position

In the musical notation, here as elsewhere in the book, the two notes are simply written one above the other, as if they were played simultaneously. This is to avoid unnecessary complexity in the notation.

The sequence ends with another *compás* of rhythm, after the music has returned to the major key.

Sequence 4: third FALSETA (ESCOBILLA)

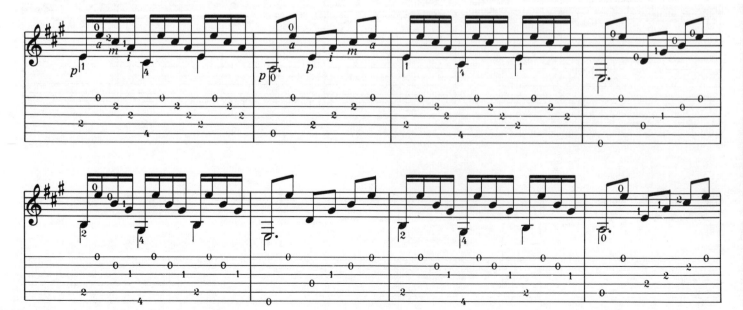

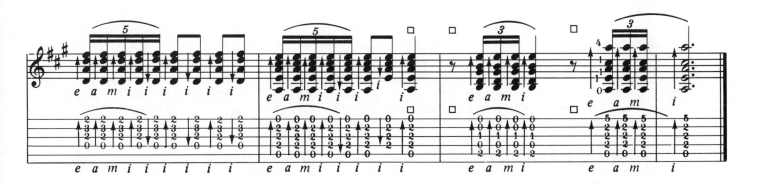

Sequence 4 *(continued)*

This very traditional and tuneful *falseta* is an excellent exercise for the four-note 'back' *arpegio* played with **p a m i**. The right thumb plays the melody notes *apoyando* on the bass strings. Then **a m i** play *tirando* on strings 1, 2 and 3, respectively.

The important aim here is to keep the rhythm of each *arpegio* absolutely regular, making sure that the fingers strike with equal force, their movement coming from the knuckle joints, the hand not moving, the wrist relaxed. The four notes of each *arpegio* should be evenly spaced in time, without a delay after the thumbstroke.

The left hand fingers hold down their chord positions (of A or E7) while the 4th finger moves to stop the notes of the melody which are not part of the chord being held down. If your left hand position is a good one, the 4th finger will have only a short distance to travel onto the strings it stops, since it will be naturally positioned over the fourth fret-space close to the strings.

The final chord introduces a new chord of A major. The left-hand position is shown in photo 6.5 and in the accompanying chord diagram.

The straightened first finger actually stops the four top strings at the 2nd fret, but only the notes made on strings 2, 3 and 4 are sounded in the chord. The first string is stopped by the little finger at the 5th fret.

This way of using the first finger of the left hand to stop several strings at a single fret is an example of the technique of *Barré,* which is described in detail in Lesson 8.

6.5 A major chord with A on 1st string.

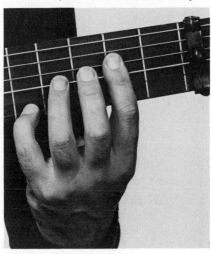

Elements of Flamenco 6 Choosing a guitar

The experienced guitarist will look for many points when assessing a guitar, whatever its price. But two features stand out above all others, namely the facility for right and left hands the instrument allows him and its sound.

It is well worth going to some trouble to find a more expert player or a teacher whose advice you can trust about any guitar you are thinking of buying. He will know more about weighing up the strengths and weaknesses of a guitar, but only you can make the final decision about whether it suits you. If you are going to buy new from a dealer, find one who has a special interest in Flamenco.

The major details of workmanship which require attention include the following:

First appearances. Guitar manufacturers know how susceptible buyers are to beautiful decoration and a glossy finish when they come to choose a guitar. Just as with a car, however, it is what is under the bonnet that counts, and an attractive finish gives little or no clue about how well the guitar is going to play and sound.

The instrument should show careful and accurate workmanship and the use of appropriate and well-seasoned woods. Even in the cheapest guitars one must demand proper timbers and internal strutting. Veneered laminates must be absolutely avoided. The better *tapas* are made of close-grained German spruce or Canadian cedar and both halves should match closely. An even grain should be evident in other woods. Major defects like a sunken *tapa*, a bridge-saddle that is about to come off or a warped neck should be obvious.

The neck should be absolutely straight. Its rounded curvature must be smoothly finished, with a breadth and curvature that feel comfortable all the way along the fingerboard. Check for any sign of warping. Do not buy a warped guitar. The wood used may have been too young or the guitar may have suffered from central-heating or other extremes of temperature or humidity.

The fingerboard, a separate piece of hardwood applied to the neck, must be perfectly flat. Ebony is best. The frets should be well-fitted into slots, with bevelled edges and no jagged projections which snag the left hand fingers. Test by sliding the left hand along both edges of the fingerboard. The note at each fret on every string must be played to detect any excessive buzzes resulting from uneven height of frets. A scale-length longer than the normal 66 cms (from nut to bridge) is likely to feel uncomfortable for those with smaller hands.

The intonation must be true at all frets. You can test this by playing octave harmonics at the 12th fret on each string to ensure that the note coincides with the pitch of the note when the string is firmly stopped against the 12th fret. Check notes at all frets and play octaves (e.g. E's at 2nd fret on fourth string and open first string; D's on 10th fret of first string and 12th of fourth string etc.). The open strings must, of course, be very accurately tuned for these tests.

Responsiveness is a difficult quality to define in words, but it refers to the immediacy of sound production by the *tapa*. In good guitars there is a definite resonance to be heard when the sides and back are gently knocked with the back of a finger. A good flamenco guitar has a feeling about it of being imbued with a kind of nervous energy and tension that makes it respond instantly to the slightest touch on the strings. The timbers are thin, hard and immediately alive with sound and there is no sense of slackness or heaviness in the wood.

Flamenco guitars, especially those with peg heads, may feel very light in weight but this is not a good guide to quality. A very light guitar can be bad and a rather heavy one could be magnificent.

Many of the finest guitars need considerable time to warm up before they can produce their true brilliance and vibrant intensity of sound. The wood resonates less well when it is cold. Nearly all guitars improve for a time with age, but the process has limits and a flamenco guitar may pass its best by 10 or 20 years of age. For a guitar to be well and truly played in, so that its initial coarseness and 'woodiness' have gone, it requires lots of strong playing of all its notes over a period of months or even a year or two. A guitar that has been long unplayed or has been accustomed to being only gently tickled cannot give of its best.

The action of the guitar should be examined and the range of modification possible by altering the height of the *huesos* ('bones', i.e. the nut and bridge-saddle). The 'action' of the guitar, which determines its ease of playing, is made up of several factors, including the responsiveness of the soundboard, the tension of the strings and their height from the fingerboard and soundboard. Too low or soft an action will cause excessive buzz at all but minimal volume. Too high or hard an action will make the guitar sound more 'classical' and will make it more of an effort to play. Paradoxically there are some guitars which buzz less if the action is lowered. Some degree of buzz is needed to get the right sort of ringing attack in the sound of the *rasgueo*, but the individual notes of the guitar, particularly on the higher strings, must give a clear and unfuzzy sound.

The beginner may be attracted by the very low or soft action of a guitar since it offers greater ease of playing, but there are reasons which may make a harder action a better choice. Such an action may favour greater projection and clarity of tone, besides helping to develop the necessary strength in the fingers.

It is, of course, essential to ensure that the guitar is fitted with strings of the highest quality and most appropriate tension. These must be tuned exactly to concert pitch and be in good condition, otherwise valid assessment of the sound quality and action is not possible.

Balance of sound quality and loudness should be distributed as equally as possible between bass, mid-range and treble, not only with the open strings but all over the fingerboard, with all notes having adequate projection, volume and sustain. A good bass is more commonly found than a clear singing treble, and if you are not careful, you may allow yourself to be over-impressed by the potency of the bass notes, particularly if the strings are brand new. The treble is very important in Flamenco. It is particularly in regard to the balance of sound quality that the really exceptional guitar can be differentiated from the merely very good.

Play chromatic scales all the way up every string to hear the sound of every note. If you are choosing a guitar from several of the same make in a shop, try every one of them because differences in sound quality and action may be marked.

When you are testing a guitar for sound you have to be very careful not to be misled by resonance from the surroundings. Uncarpetted rooms with a very resonant acoustic can give you the impression you are getting much more sound from the guitar than you really are. To test the guitar itself, unaided by the surroundings, you need a very 'dry', unresonant acoustic such as you would get in a well-furnished sitting-room.

Loudness is not at all the same thing as quality or projection. A guitar with real quality, even if it seems quieter, can project further and more clearly. A new guitar with new strings can sound tremendously loud and powerful at first only to reveal its poor quality of tone once you have listened to it more critically, particularly when the strings are a little older and its brashness has faded. A good flamenco guitar retains most of its brilliance even with ancient strings.

Pegs or machine-heads must be well-fitting and easily adjusted. The best pegs are made of ebony. An application of an extremely small amount of dry soap or French chalk may prevent a tendency to stick in older pegs. Excessive wear in the cogs of machine-heads indicates poor quality materials; the winding action must be positive and immediate. For most players, other qualities of the guitar will be more important in determining choice than the question of whether it has pegs or machines.

Nut and bridge-saddle should be of bone and not plastic. The slots at the nut must be accurately cut to allow the strings to lie in a single plane. No wear should be visible at the bridge-saddle. The height of the *huesos* can be raised if necessary, by thin strips of plastic or card.

The innards. Much of the most important construction of the guitar is out of sight. If you are really obsessional about it, you can inspect the system of fan-strutting used by means of a dentist's mirror. At least there should not be any excessive glue visible through the sound-hole.

The label. Although you may well have looked at the label first, this may sometimes be the last thing you should be influenced by. One occasionally hears stories of people buying guitars which have had false labels, cannibalised from broken instruments, stuck in them. A very much commoner, and entirely legitimate, practice is for guitars bearing the name of a famous maker to be made by apprentices or a factory. The famous name may then be simply a brand name of the marketing firm. If you want to be sure you have a guitar hand-made by the individual maker himself, the only way is to make yourself thoroughly acquainted with that maker's own system of labelling the guitars of different grades sold under his name. Almost always it will only be the most expensive model which is made personally by him or by an apprentice under his direct supervision. Slightly cheaper models may be the work of apprentices or may be, like the cheapest, the product of a separate workshop, or factory using semi-mass-production methods.

Going for the best

The best flamenco guitars are as individual as beautiful women, and as difficult to choose between. One's relationship with the instrument is a very personal and individual thing that has to feel right. In a word, the player must be able to *dominate* a guitar.

Constructional differences between guitars include variations of scale-length (some players prefer a scale shorter than 66 cms), width of fingerboard and overall action. Professional players commonly ask for guitars to be built to their own requirements.

Some would-be purchasers have been disappointed to find that even a visit to the *guitarrero* (guitar-maker) does little to reduce the months or years of waiting that may be necessary if one is to obtain a new guitar by the maker of one's choice. Certainly if the *guitarrero* has any for offer for over-the-counter sale to a stranger they are unlikely to be of the very best.

The cheaper guitar

So-called 'Flamenco' guitars are available at a wide range of prices, but the cheapest guitars sold under that title are often not worth the money. To obtain anything like the real flamenco tone and action you usually have to go at least to the middle price bracket or above. Even paying a lot for a flamenco guitar that is less than the very best is no guarantee of obtaining those elusive tonal qualities so vital to Flamenco. In general, therefore, it may be best to buy a guitar with reasonable playing facility to start on, even if it is a cheap classical model from Valencia or Japan which has to be fitted with *golpeadores*, and then to wait until you can afford a really good new or second-hand instrument.

There are some excellent medium-priced instruments about but it is hard to generalise. To give just one example, some guitars by Ricardo Sanchis are good, at about a quarter of the price of the most expensive. Some of the Japanese guitars are now attractive and may, if not too expensive, be very adequate to start on.

It is well to remember that guitars are still relatively cheap musical instruments and that the very best of them provide a good protection against inflation. New players often buy too expensive a guitar at the outset only to be disappointed when they can compare it with first-class, and often only slightly more expensive, guitars made by the top *guitarreros*. A really good make can be a much better and cheaper buy second-hand than new ones of mediocre quality.

LESSON 7   More Soleares

The following short solo sequence of Soleares is more advanced than the first in that the rhythm passages make extensive use of the 5-stroke *rasgueo*. Besides giving you some more *falsetas* to increase your repertoire in this vital *toque*, a major aim of the piece is to help you get these 5-stroke *rasgueos* fitting in accurately with the rhythm of the *compás*. They should not be hurried. On the recording you will be able to hear clearly each of the 5 strokes with the fingers.

 CASSETTE: LESSON 7, SECOND SOLEARES

First COMPÁS (repeated)
The introduction is a traditional *compás* based on E major chords played with the thumb, which are held down by the left hand during an extended *ligado* on the 4th string. After the chord is sounded, notes are played *ligado* on the 4th string by fingers 2 and 3 'hammering on' and 'pulling off'.

COMPASES 3-5
Two new chords are introduced. The first, derived from the chord position of Fmaj7 with D sharp added on the second string at the fourth fret, is shown in 7.1 and the accompanying chord diagram. It occurs on beat 9 of the fourth *compás*.

The other new chord (on beat 3 of the fifth *compás*) is a version of F major on just the lower strings. The fingers adopt the position shown in 7.2 on the bottom four strings. In the solo, the thumb strikes only the bottom three.

There are three traditional *falsetas*. Comments on the second and third follow on p.55.

FALSETA 1
is played with the thumb, *apoyando*. The *falseta* is punctuated by the *arpegio* phrase you have met before. The syncopated accents, marked in the music, need careful attention. They add interest to a simple melody and are an essential feature of the *falseta*.

(See Text)

7.1 F maj 7 position with D sharp added on 2nd string.

F major

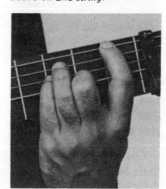

7.2 F major position on lower four strings.

Second Soleares

Cejilla at 2nd fret

FALSETA 1

FALSETA 2

FALSETA 3

C7

D7

FALSETA 2

starts with *arpegios* and the ending is played with thumb and *ligados*.

FALSETA 3

is played largely in tenths and octaves with thumb *apoyando* and index *tirando*, as already described. The left hand has to move to higher fret-positions. Two new chords are introduced, D7 and C7, indicated in the music. The same chord shape is used for both chords, at the third and first fret-positions respectively. The chord shape is shown in photo 7.3 alongside the chord diagrams for D7 and C7.

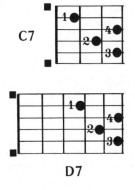

C7

D7

7.3 C7 position.

Elements of Flamenco 7   Guitarreros

The design of the flamenco guitar, in both the form and materials by which it is known today, takes origin from the innovations of the great Antonio Torres of Almería (d.1892). Before Torres the guitars of the day, called *guitarras de tablao*, were smaller, shallower and much less powerful in sound. Torres introduced larger body dimensions (the *plantilla Torres*) and a deeper body, together with other improvements in construction and materials and a clear differentiation between flamenco and classical instruments. His influence and that of succeeding great *guitarreros* who introduced further innovations and refinements can be traced through successive generations of master and apprentice.

Manuel Ramirez of Madrid (d.1916), brother of José Ramirez I who was a famous maker of the older-style instrument, adopted and extended Torres' techniques and passed them on to his apprentices, Santos Hernandez, Domingo Esteso and Modesto Borreguero.

Santos Hernandez (d.1942) achieved prestigious status as Spain's most sought-after *guitarrero* and his instruments today are prized collectors' items. He was, it is said, totally secretive about his working methods and refused to have an apprentice. After his death, however, his widow maintained his shop, employing Marcel Barbero (d.1956), who thereby had access to Santos Hernandez' plans and tools.

José Ramirez II, nephew of Manuel and son of José I, had earlier taught Marcelo Barbero and his own son José Ramirez III. The line of succession from Barbero passed on to Arcangel Fernandez, who is still one of Madrid's finest makers of flamenco guitars, and through him to the young Marcelo Barbero Hijo.

José Ramirez III has achieved international fame (and many imitators) for his classical guitars, especially admired for their fine qualities of tone and finish and for their remarkable consistency. He has also made some fine flamenco instruments, particularly in the new style of the *guitarra negra* with rosewood sides and back. Several of today's leading makers have developed their craft in his Madrid workshop and then have gone on to establish themselves independently, notably Manuel Contreras, Feliz Manzanero and Paulino Bernabé. Best known for their classical guitars, these *guitarreros* have also made some excellent flamenco instruments.

Domingo Esteso, (d.1937) hardly less prestigious a maker of flamenco guitars than Santos Hernandez and a much more prolific one, made the guitars played in the '30's by many professional players, including Niño Ricardo. His tradition has been maintained and developed by his three nephews, Faustino, Mariano and Julio under the name Sobrinos de Domingo Esteso (or more recently Hermanos Conde). For years now their guitars have been the preferred choice of many professional players. Their highly distinctive qualities of warmth and sweetness of tone combined with a superb ringing vibrancy make them the aristocrats of the flamenco guitar, easily recognised on many recordings.

Two outstanding makers of flamenco guitar in Córdoba are Manuel Reyes, largely self-taught but powerfully influenced by Barbero's ideas, and Miguel Rodriguez.

Today there are several very talented *guitarreros* among the younger generation. Especially worthy of mention is Gerundino Fernandez of Almería whose flamenco guitars possess an extraordinarily potent and distinctive 'flamenconess', combining a singing purity of tone with amazing immediacy of response. A young man, totally dedicated to the guitar and Flamenco, he expresses in his guitars all that is purest and most 'earthy' in Flamenco, a quality almost too fiercely lamenting to appeal to concert audiences used to the gently mellow sounds of the classical guitar. Their projection and brilliance are quite remarkable.

Others among today's makers in Spain who have made good flamenco instruments include Francisco Barba (Sevilla), Antonio Marin Montero (Granada), Jeronimo Peña Fernandez and the brothers Alvarez (Madrid).

The guitars shown in the photographs in this book are, as can be recognised from their distinctive carving on the head, by Gerundino Fernandez (the guitar with pegs) and by Sobrinos de Domingo Esteso. Guitars by both these makers are heard on the cassette-recording.

LESSON 8   Barré and Double Arpegio

This lesson introduces two important techniques. The first, for the left hand, is the index finger *barré*, then for the right hand, the *double arpegio*. The two will be combined in an attractive exercise taught by Maestro Esquembre, a renowned guitar-teacher in Madrid. The exercise, which is recorded on the cassette, also illustrates left hand action in changing chords in higher fret-positions.

The BARRÉ

To make a *barré*, the left index finger is placed straight across all six strings, stopping them behind the same fret. In this way it acts like a movable *cejilla* to provide a basis for chords and melodies in higher fret-positions than we have so far been using. It allows the other fingers to adopt similar chord shapes to ones already described, with the difference that notes previously played on open strings are now stopped by the first finger and the pitch of the whole chord is raised.

We start with the chord of F major, shown in photos 8.1 and 8.2. The chord diagram shows that it is the same chord shape as the E major chord, only moved up one fret higher on all six strings. The index finger *barré* means that fingers 2, 3 and 4 now stop the positions taken by 1, 2 and 3 in the E major chord you have previously learned.

The chord diagram for the F major chord is:

Notation of the BARRÉ

In notation, the letter C (for *'cejilla'*) above the chord is the conventional way of indicating an index finger *barré* across all six strings. The Roman numeral which follows indicates the number of the fret behind which the first finger is placed. Thus, F major will be written as shown on the right.

Often it is not necessary for the index finger to stop all six strings. In the last chord of the Alegrías in Lesson 6 for instance, only the top four strings need to be stopped by the index, which therefore only extends far enough across the fingerboard to stop the number required (as shown in photo 6.5). This is often rather ambiguously called a *half-barré* and may be indicated by the symbol ½C, even though, strictly, this should mean that only three strings are stopped by the *barré*. A more accurate method, used here, is to indicate the exact number of strings stopped by the index in the form of a fraction to base 6. Thus the symbol 4/6 C means that the *barré* extends over the four top strings only.

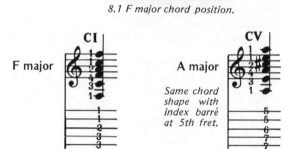

F major

8.1 F major chord position.

Economy of effort

Beginners often find the *barré* painfully difficult because they approach it in the wrong way and exert a lot of unnecessary effort which quickly causes spasm of the fingers. In fact, not much pressure is needed to stop all six strings firmly so that each can give a clear note.

Start by laying the straightened index finger across the strings immediately behind the first fret as lightly as you can. For this to be easily done, the left hand must be in a good position, with the wrist relaxed and held forward at the sort of angle with the forearm shown in photo 8.2. Bend the other fingers into their positions on the strings behind the appropriate frets and then apply just enough pressure between thumb and fingers to bring all six strings firmly against the frets, so that they are securely stopped. Sound all six strings with a slow downward sweep of the right thumb to give you a good note from each string in turn from 6th to 1st.

If you find yourself getting discouraged by an initial inability to obtain clean-sounding notes from the strings, you will find it easier if you move the same chord shape up to a higher fret-position where the frets are closer together. With the *barré* at the 5th fret, for instance, you will be playing a chord of A major (photo 8.3).

8.2 Posture of left hand and wrist for **barré**.

There are a few more points to note about the *barré*:

- the pressure of the *barré* must not be exerted by pulling the left hand towards you with the arm. The arm stays relaxed.

- the position of the thumb (shown opposite the index in photo 8.2) is important because the pressure needed comes primarily from a squeezing action between thumb and index.

- Note where the tip of the index finger lies in relation to the fingerboard (see photo 8.1). Do not push it over too far towards you.

- You will feel discomfort in the thumb muscles lying between thumb and index finger when you first maintain a *barré* for more than a brief spell of time. With practice, however, you will soon be able to hold the *barré* down comfortably even for long periods.

- Once you have got used to the feel of the *barré*, you will find it possible to change fret-positions and chord shapes quickly up and down the fingerboard. Our slow motion approach here is just designed to get the left hand into the way of adopting a good basic position.

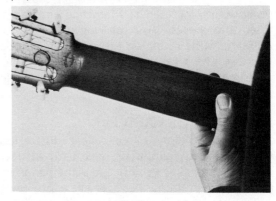

8.3 A major chord position with barré. (Cejilla at 2nd fret).

8.4 Thumb stays in middle of neck with barré in higher position.

Double ARPEGIO

This right hand technique, developed to a level of great virtuosity by Don Ramón Montoya, is extensively used in Flamenco to give an intricate, beautifully rounded sound to *arpegios*.

Each *arpegio* has 6 notes, a thumb *apoyando* on a bass note being followed by **i m a m i** *tirando* in turn on 3 adjacent higher strings. This is shown in the simple example below, using the chord of E major. Each group of notes is written as a sextuplet, with the figure 6 indicating that the 6 notes of each *arpegio* occupy the duration of one beat.

The art of *double arpegio* depends on playing the notes sounded by **p i m a m i** in sequence at perfectly regular intervals, with each note equally loud. The thumb plays a melody line in the bass.

Try the exercise extremely slowly at first, concentrating on ensuring absolute evenness of timing and volume before you try to increase the speed.

When the *4-note arpegio* was introduced earlier it was suggested you should (though only as a practice exercise) flex the fingers until their tips contact the ball of the thumb. The same technique here will help you to get the feel of the finger movements needed.

Ex.13

An example of Double Arpegio in Soleares

When you can play the preceding exercise evenly and in regular timing, you can aim to introduce the *double arpegio* in place of the *4-note arpegio* to give a richer texture of sound in the second *falseta* of the Soleares of Lesson 7, as follows:

The example (which has not been separately recorded on the cassette) demonstrates the kind of way that the *arpegio* may be used in Flamenco and the speed needed for its execution. You will find many further examples in later solo pieces. Your playing will need to become fluent and quite fast if you are to fit the *arpegio* into the *compás*, while retaining the smooth *redondo* ('rounded') quality which is so essential to good *arpegio*-playing. The exercise which follows employs the right hand fingering of the *double arpegio* at a much slower pace than would be required for Soleares. It will help you develop the control and fluency necessary if you are to play the *arpegio* well at the faster speeds.

Esquembre's exercise

The exercise below is an excellent illustration of the kind of study material, derived from classical guitar technique, which flamenco guitarists have used in developing the technical virtuosity needed for solo concert playing. The demands it makes on left and right hands and the importance of obtaining a good tone from the guitar make it a good exercise to practise every day. For each *double arpegio* phrase the left hand holds down a chord position. The sixth note of each *arpegio* preceding a change of chord position by the left hand must be given its full time-value.

CASSETTE: LESSON 8, EXERCISE IN DOUBLE ARPEGIO AND BARRÉ

Do not cut the note short by moving the left hand too soon, or you will interrupt the smooth flow of the music. The left hand changes of chord will have to be performed rapidly in order to keep the rhythm even throughout.

Ex. 14   No cejilla

58

Changing chords with the left hand

The only way to become adept at moving the left hand from one chord shape to another at the same or a different fret-position is to practise the change repeatedly, keeping the rhythm slow enough so that you do not disrupt it at all when the chord change occurs.

The fingers should stay flexed over the frets, being lifted as short a distance as possible from the fingerboard as the move is made in order to maintain maximum economy of movement. Quite often you will find that one or more fingers can retain contact with the string during the move if they are to stop the same string in the new chord.

If you adopt this energy-saving and time-saving approach from the start, practising each move carefully in advance so that the fingers move the shortest possible distance between one position and the next and the thumb always stays in contact with the neck, you will soon develop good habits and a neat-looking left hand.

To start with you will not find it easy to move all the fingers at the same time into their new positions. It may be necessary, therefore, to place the fingers on the frets in rapid succession so that the strings are stopped in the order they are to be sounded. With practice, however, all the fingers will move into place simultaneously.

Give these all-important principles of efficient left hand action enough thought and practice early on and economical movements will become so natural and quick as to look and feel effortless. Your fingers will simply know by themselves where to go, without your needing even to look at them.

Elements of Flamenco 8   History (1)

In spite of extensive research into the origins of the flamenco arts there is still no general agreement about exactly how Flamenco came into being. The intermingling of Moorish and Christian, gypsy and non-gypsy strands in the evolution over centuries of the Flamenco that we know in Andalucía today cannot be unravelled so that one can confidently assess the contribution of each. Legends abound but indisputable facts are few.

The word 'Flamenco'
Even the origins of the word 'Flamenco' are controversial. Probably of Arabic derivation, it is found in popular usage at the beginning of the 19th century as a slang term for an arrogant or affected person. Later it came to designate the gypsies *(gitanos)* of Andalucía, and only later still was it applied to their songs and dances. The use of the general term *Cante Flamenco* to denote a type of Andalusian song derived from both gypsy and non-gypsy origins seems to have become well established only in the second half of the 19th century.

The early roots
Any theory about Flamenco must explain why it is a uniquely *Andaluz* (Andalusian) phenomenon. It began as a music of the poorer people, so that its emergence is poorly documented. There is little detailed information before the latter half of the 19th century. You will have often heard it said that the *gitanos* first gave voice to the *Cante*. Certainly they have been particularly identified with the performance of such essential *cantes* as Soleares, Seguiriyas, Tangos and Bulerías. But the argument as to how much they actually created still goes on, at times heatedly.

These itinerant people had arrived in Spain in the 15th century at the end of their long migration from northern India. After centuries of persecution, the *gitanos* of Andalucía had become settled in communities which were to become particularly associated with the genesis of Flamenco, especially the Triana in Sevilla and gypsy quarters in Cádiz, Jerez de la Frontera, Granada, Málaga, Ronda and other towns and villages of Andalucía. In their daily lives they lived close to the Mozarabic descendants of the Moors expelled en masse from Spain in 1492, and with the poorer classes of the older indigenous communities. They were renowned for their talents as singers and dancers, and one may presume that they brought musical elements from their own Indian heritage, as well as contributing their style of voice production, poetically attributed to *el dolor en la garganta* ('the grief in the throat'), so characteristic of the *voz rajada* (cracked voice) of the *cantaor* (singer). The *gitano* influence is evident, too, in the language of the *coplas*, with its many references to the personal tragedies and oppression of their lives and their occupations in the fields and as silversmiths and blacksmiths.

But what music was there in Andalucía already, derived from Moorish and even earlier Christian, Judaic and North African sources? There were, after all, gypsies in many other parts of Spain, so that we must look to other sources for the particularly *Andaluz* flavour of Flamenco, and the origins of its characteristic modal scale. It is possible that the role of the gypsies has been somewhat romanticised and that too little has been made of other cultures to the south and east of the Mediterranean, revealed in close affinities of form and phrasing between Flamenco and the music of Islam. Certainly there were pre-gypsy Arabic songs such as the Fandango, and others too which were adapted and popularised by *Andaluces* besides the *gitanos*.

The main birth-place of Flamenco was within an area of Andalucía centred on Jerez de la Frontera and extending to include Sevilla, Cádiz, Granada, Málaga and Ronda. It is bordered to the north by the ancient limits of the Moorish conquest of Spain. In this extraordinary crucible of musical alchemy were fused the elements, including Moorish, Mozarabic, Islamic, Hebraic, Hindu, Persian, Byzantine and Greek liturgical, which together made a uniquely *Andaluz* amalgam of musical culture. Somehow it became transmuted into the pure gold of Flamenco.

Further evolution of Flamenco
The processes of absorption and intermingling, by which Flamenco incorporated many forms of *Andaluz* folk-music as well as, later on, some South American songs and rhythms have been continuing ones. In turn Flamenco has influenced the wider sphere of Spanish song and dance. While the trend has lately been to look north and west-ward, towards jazz and European popular music for newer sources of inspiration, it is probably much truer to the early traditions of Flamenco and to its special capacities for musical expression to look south and eastward, to the world of Islam in North Africa and Asia Minor.

LESSON 9   Fandangos de Huelva

The Fandango has Arabic roots which reach back in time to the early beginnings of Flamenco during the Moors' occupation of southern Spain. From its birthplace in Andalucía this ancient form of song and dance spread throughout Spain, and over centuries it has evolved in different ways according to the influence of different regions, localities and individual performers. In the north it was the basis for the Jota, while in the south it gave origin to the Rondeña, the Malagueña, the Granadina, the Taranta, Minera and Cartagenera.

Fandangos and fandanguillos are sung all over Andalucía and are traditionally known by local names. The performances of much-promoted *'fandangueros'* became so popular during the earlier decades of this century that for a time the Fandango nearly eclipsed all other styles of Flamenco.

Today, from the viewpoint of the guitarist, we can distinguish two main types of Fandango. On the one hand are those highly expressive Fandangos, like the *Fandangos Grandes*, which belong primarily to the *Cante*: these allow considerable individual freedom within the *compás*. On the other hand are the strongly rhythmic Fandangos which can be both danced and sung. These are particularly associated with the province and town of Huelva.

In the *Cante por Fandangos*, the themes of the *coplas* are extremely varied, ranging from tragedies of disillusion and betrayal in the more serious styles all the way to ironic humour and absurdity in the most light-hearted. Often, especially in the *Fandangos Grandes*, the lines (*'letras'*) of each *copla* lead up to a telling point, a dramatic climax or a humorous punch-line at the end. The audience responds with a chorus of *'Olé's*, while the guitarist begins an interlude of *rasgueo* and *falsetas* which ushers in the new drama of the next *copla*. The communication between singer, guitarist and audience can be incredibly intense, a very moving experience.

The COMPÁS of Fandangos de Huelva

The *compás* of Fandangos de Huelva is lively, emphatic and unvarying. Its rhythmic structure, compellingly simple when one hears the music, is essentially straightforward. Yet many students find it one of the harder *toques* to understand. There is only one aspect which needs special clarification, and that is the relationship of the *falsetas* to the intervening passages of rhythm *rasgueo*.

Basically the rhythm is made up of 12-beat *compases* with a recurring pattern of accented beats which you will hear clearly when you listen to the music. In the case of Soleares we were able to state which numbered beats carry the accents of the rhythm, but the *compás* of Fandangos is different and does not lend itself so well to this simple approach. It can be confusing to try to assign the accents to particular numbered beats because, as is described in detail below, passages of rhythmic *rasgueo* and *falsetas* are best counted in different ways. Many *falsetas* have 14 beats in their final resolution (ending phrase) and they start two beats earlier than might be expected. Those *falsetas* which derive directly from *coplas* of the *cante*, on the other hand, fit more simply into the recurring pattern of 12 beats, without the need for a longer ending or early beginning.

The method of counting the *compás* is described here in detail so that you can study it at leisure. It will be important for you to understand the underlying principles, but they are unlikely to mean much until you have gained some familiarity with the music. You may well prefer, therefore, to skip the following section on the two types of *falseta* and to go straight on to studying the recorded solo and the written music. You can then return later to the theory of the *compás*. Once you have started to play Fandangos it will all seem much clearer.

The two types of FALSETA

We could count Fandangos all the way through in consecutive sequences *(compases)* counted 1 to 12. The phrasing of the *rasgueo* rhythm would fit in well with this method but we would find that the commonest type of *falseta*, which we will call here a Type I *falseta*, starts with its first accented beat on a count of 11. Rather than counting the *falseta* 11, 12, 1, 2, etc. it is far simpler to count it in *compases* of 1 to 12 since it is made up, characteristically, of musical phrases 6 beats long. To do this, we will have to count the *rasgueo compás* which immediately precedes the *falseta* as 1 to 10 only, so that we can start again from 1 to 12 at the beginning of the *falseta*.

But why should this *compás* of *rasgueo* before the *falseta* have to be two beats shorter than the other *compases* of *rasgueo*? The answer lies in the way these *falsetas* end, with a resolution which needs one extended *compás* counted 1 to 14. It is this long ending phrase which accounts for the *falseta* starting 'early' after a *rasgueo compás* of only 10 beats. After the *falseta* the *rasgueo* then resumes again from 1 to 12 (or 1 to 10 if another Type 1 *falseta* immediately follows).

We can summarise the counting as follows:

Type I FALSETAS *(commonest)*

| Rhythmic *rasgueo* in *compases* of 1 to 12 | One shorter *compás* of *rasgueo* before *falseta*, counted 1 to 10 | Type I *falseta* in *compases* of 1 to 12 (subdivided into 6-beat phrases) | Ending of *falseta*, counted as a *compás* of 1 to 14 | Rhythmic *rasgueo* in *compases* of 1 to 12 | etc. |

Falsetas which are melodies of *coplas* of the *Cante* we can call Type II *Falsetas*. They are much less numerous in the guitarist's repertoire than Type I *falsetas* and easier to count. Their melodies are phrased in lines of 12 beats duration, without the extended final *compás* (counted 1 to 14) of Type I *falsetas*. The counting, therefore, is very straightforward and may be summarised as follows:

Type II FALSETAS *(coplas)*

| Rhythmic *rasgueo* in *compases* of 1 to 12 | Type II *falseta* in *compases* of 1 to 12 | Rhythmic *rasgueo* in *compases* of 1 to 12 | etc. |

The notation
There is a problem about writing down Fandangos in such a way that the accents of the rhythm can be easily grasped from the notation. This is not, of course, a problem for flamencos because they do not learn from written music. Most transcribers have adopted a fast 3/4 time, where each beat of the bar corresponds to one counted beat of the *compás*. This method obscures the all-important accentuation of the rhythm, so a slow 3/4 time is used instead here which makes the accents coincide with the first, second and third beats of the bar. The music is slower than it may look at first: one counted number corresponds to one half-beat in the bar.

The solo

The solo which follows is first played on the cassette at normal speed. Fandangos de Huelva can be played at a faster speed than you will hear, but the speed at which it is recorded was chosen as being fast enough to convey the typical rhythmic pulse of the *toque*, without being too fast to follow in written music. After the whole solo is played, the introduction with *rasgueo* and the first *falseta* is heard again at a slow speed in order to give you a clear understanding of the rhythm, the way the more complicated Type I *falseta* is counted and the way the counting fits in with the 3/4 time of the written notation.

 **CASSETTE: LESSON 9, FANDANGOS**

Introduction and FALSETA I: In the slower version you will hear a rhythmic introduction with *rasgueo* and down- and upstrokes (A to B in the music), a traditional Type I *falseta* (B to C) made up of typical 6-beat *arpegio* phrases, then more *rasgueo* rhythm. Try to play this through with even rhythm and strong emphasis on the accents before you attempt to proceed further with the rest of the solo, for which you will need to go back on the cassette to the recording of the whole piece at normal speed. A new chord of G major, fingered in the notation, is played on the lower four strings on beat 7 of the rhythm *compases*.

INTRODUCTION & 1st FALSETA, SLOWLY

FALSETA 2 is the melody of a traditional *copla*, so that it is an example of Type II. Note the different counting and the absence of the extended ending. The melody is played in the key of A major, changing to A minor in the final phrase as it resolves back to the usual Phrygian mode of Fandangos. The melody notes are played *apoyando* by index and middle finger while the bass notes are played *tirando* by the thumb.

Brief comments on *falsetas* 3 and 4 follow the written music.

FANDANGOS DE HUELVA

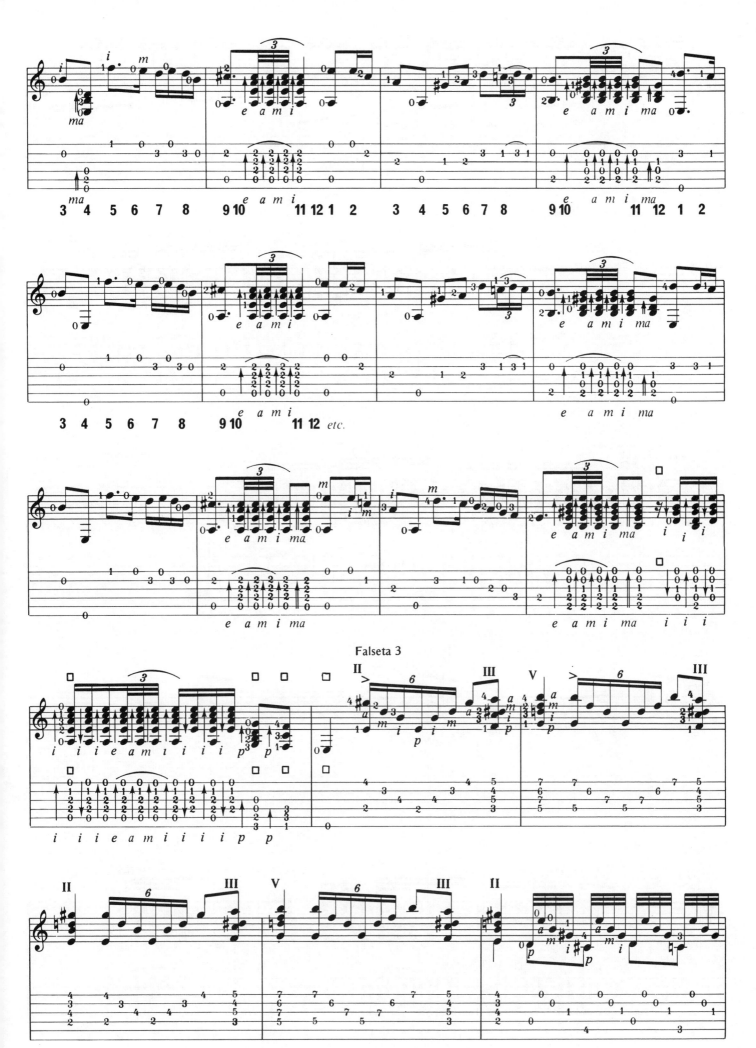

Falseta 3

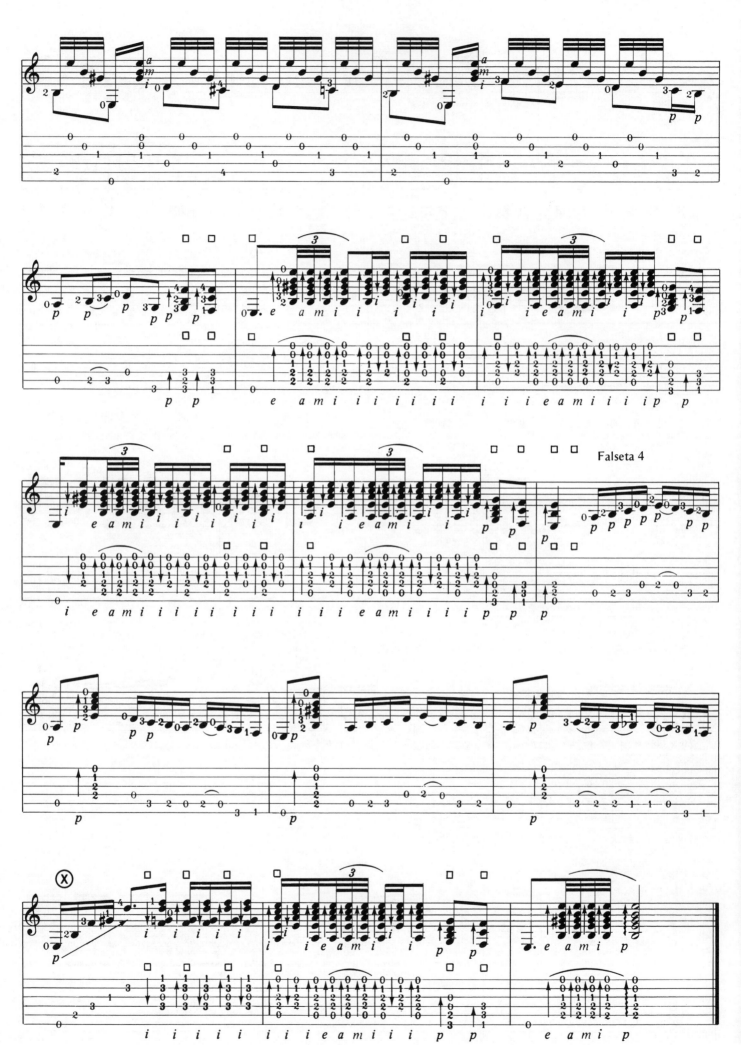

Falseta 4

64

FALSETA 3. Here the left hand adopts a chord shape (E7) on the top four strings which is maintained when the hand is moved to higher fret-positions (F7 then G7) and back again. There is a new right hand *arpegio* pattern: the fingering is shown in the music. 4-string chords also occur in which four strings are sounded simultaneously. Thumb and three fingers play *tirando*, the fingers moving from the knuckle joints without movement of the hand as a whole. The hand is not pulled away from the strings but stays relaxed while fingers and thumb do the work. The tips of the fingers move in lines directed towards the ball of the thumb.

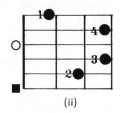

(i)

(ii)

FALSETA 4. Another traditional *falseta*, this is played *apoyando* by the thumb with the hand in the 'thumb' position. It is punctuated by thumb downstrokes, and in the left hand there is much use of *ligado* 'pulling-off'. Follow strictly the accents in the phrasing. The *falseta* ends with an ascending *arpegio* by the thumb (from the point marked X in the music) on a 'diminished' chord. The left hand fingers first take up the position shown in diagram (i) *(top right)*; the 1st finger then moves across from the 3rd to the 1st string as shown in the diagram (ii).

The final *rasgueo* which ends the solo introduces another pattern of right hand fingering. A rapid 4-stroke *rasgueo* is followed without a pause by a strong downward sweep of the thumb. The thumbstroke carries the accent of the beat. The *rasgueo* is made in one combined movement involving the fingers, thumb and wrist.

Elements of Flamenco 9   History (2) -the guitar

The early history of the guitar in Flamenco is hardly less obscure than that of the *Cante*, but its elevation to solo status is far more recent and more easily charted.

Flamenco was born of necessity, as an essential expression of the joys and sorrows of everyday life in the fields, at work and in the home. It was a music of ordinary people who shared their art among their small communities and sang together as they worked or at their leisure, accompanying themselves with the tools of their work (such as the blacksmith's hammer in the *Martinete*) or by hand-clapping and other simple forms of percussion like the beat of a stick on the ground. To begin with, these songs of everyday life and the dances that went with them on festive occasions were part of day-to-day survival or celebration, not highly polished performances to instrumental accompaniment. The guitar, therefore, was not an essential or even an important part of this early Flamenco.

A story often repeated is that the flamenco guitar came about by the gypsies' adaptation of 'classical' guitar techniques to suit the accompaniment of the flamenco *Cante*, its use growing in popularity and sophistication along with the wealth and status of flamenco performers. But this simple tale seems likely to be all too simple and perhaps gravely mistaken. The most distinctive features of older-style flamenco guitar-playing are worlds apart from 'classical' guitar techniques. The percussive *rasgueos* and accented phrasing seem, instead, to have close similarities to techniques heard in Arabic music for the *'ud* and other stringed instruments whose origins date back to the time of the Moors. Rather than being an offshoot of classical guitar development, flamenco techniques seem likely to be derived far more directly from early Mozarabic and other ancient *Andaluz* instrumental music. Once again, the *gitanos'* role may have been over-emphasised.

Guitarists
It was during the *Cafe Cantante* period of Flamenco at the end of the last century that guitarists began to achieve fame as performers in their own right, both as accompanists and soloists. *Falsetas*, initially developed as melodic interludes in the accompaniment of the *Cante*, became more elaborate and longer in the hands of individual creators. More recently, the advancing status of the solo instrument can be largely attributed to a few individual players whose virtuosity brought them recognition as concert performers and recording artists. In modern times gramophone records have played a very important role in disseminating Flamenco to a world-wide audience and in extending the fund of music available to the student of the guitar, both in Andalucía and elsewhere.

Don Ramón Montoya (1880 –1949) is revered as Flamenco's first concert recitalist and is credited with introducing technical advances such as the five-note *trémolo* and extended use of 'double' *arpegio*, together with a greater development of *picado* and other innovations. But it must not be forgotten that Don Ramón's eminence as a colossus among guitarists rested primarily on his outstanding abilities as an accompanist. Although, too, he was one of Flamenco's great creators of new *falsetas* and *rasgueos*, his playing was built onto the basis of inventions of other and earlier masters of the guitar such as Patiño and Javier Molina, whose music has passed into the guitar repertoire of Flamenco and whose innovations have been widely imitated. All have excelled in the art of accompaniment and all have grafted their *toque* firmly onto a basis of tradition.

Since Don Ramón's time two figures stand out particularly as important influences on today's younger generation of guitarists. Niño Ricardo (Manuel Serrapí) of Sevilla, who died in 1972, and Sabicas (Augustín Castellón), long resident in America, have both been especially gifted as creators, and many of their *falsetas* have been played by other guitarists or become the basis for further adaptation and development.

But it would be wrong for any history of the flamenco guitar, even the briefest, to single out only those guitarists who have been widely acclaimed. The tradition of Flamenco is like a great river formed from many tributaries. The sources of the music we now call 'traditional' cannot be attributed and there have been very many guitarists, some who have gained recognition and many more who have done so on a very small scale if at all, who have contributed something to that great current of Flamenco which inspires the guitarist of today.

LESSON 10　Sevillanas

Sevillanas are a lively and tuneful form of *Andaluz* folk-music, strongly influenced by Flamenco and now a part of it. They are said to have originated two or three centuries ago from the *seguidillas manchegas* (no connection with the flamenco Seguiriyas) of old Castile. Today a great variety of Sevillanas, to be sung, danced to and played on the guitar, have become popular throughout Andalucía, and new melodies and verses are continually being created. The strongly rhythmic *compás* is common to all.

The spirit or *aire* of Sevillanas is usually exuberant and full of *alegría* and poetic *gracia*, but some of the melodies and verses are in more serious vein. Those in the Phrygian mode have a typically flamenco character but most often the melodies are in major or minor keys so that they sound more akin to other kinds of Spanish folk-music. The pace is usually brisk, but may be slower and more deliberate in some of the serious *coplas*.

The best time to hear the most joyful Sevillanas sung and danced in all their rich variety is at Sevilla's annual *Féria* or Spring Fair, when crowds in traditional costume throng the streets and gather round the *casetas*. Many kinds of Sevillanas, including the more solemn ones, are sung along with Fandangos de Huelva by the pilgrims who join the *Romería del Rocío* on its annual progress from Sanlúcar de Barameda to Sevilla. Such expert performers as the Hermanos Toronjo and the Hermanos Reyes demonstrate the wide scope of Sevillanas on their records.

The COMPÁS of Sevillanas

The *compás* follows a strict pattern. If you bring the pulse of it alive, you will make your listeners want to get up and dance to it. You must aim to get a real bounce in your playing, even if to start with you have to play Sevillanas very slowly. The *compás* quickly becomes absorbed as part of you when you hear it often, so you would do well to listen to the recordings on the cassette many, many times, supplemented by all the records you can lay hands on.

The rhythm is harder to grasp from words or notation and, as with Fandangos de Huelva, which it closely resembles, it has often been poorly translated into written music. Again, a slow 3/4 time has been adopted here as the clearest possible way of showing accurately in notation how the rhythm is accentuated. But as with all flamenco *compases* it is important not to become preoccupied by bar-lines: it's that vital pulse of the rhythm that matters.

On the cassette, three traditional Sevillanas are first played at normal speed. These are followed by a recording of the first Sevillana of the three, played at a slow speed so that you can understand how the rhythm goes, how it can be counted and how the music has been transcribed into written notation and *cifra*. Each Sevillana has a characteristic structure which can be summarised as follows:

First, the guitar plays a rhythmic introduction counted in 6's. This is usually of *rasgueos* and down- and up-strokes but may sometimes consist of plucked chords and *arpegios*. Next comes the *Salida* (literally, 'departure'), a brief introductory passage of the melody. You will find that this is the same or very nearly the same as the last line of the melody. After a further short passage of rhythm (which is also interposed between repeats of the melody) the full melody (the *Copla*) is played three times. Variations are often introduced into it the third time it is played. At the end, the music stops abruptly. There is a brief pause, then the guitarist begins the next Sevillana, often in a different and perhaps contrasting key. Commonly, four different Sevillanas are played in succession.

Further comments on the *compás* and the solo follow the music on the next three pages.

CASSETTE: LESSON 10, THREE SEVILLANAS　　**FIRST SEVILLANA PLAYED SLOWLY WITHOUT REPEATS OF THE COPLA**

SEVILLANA 1

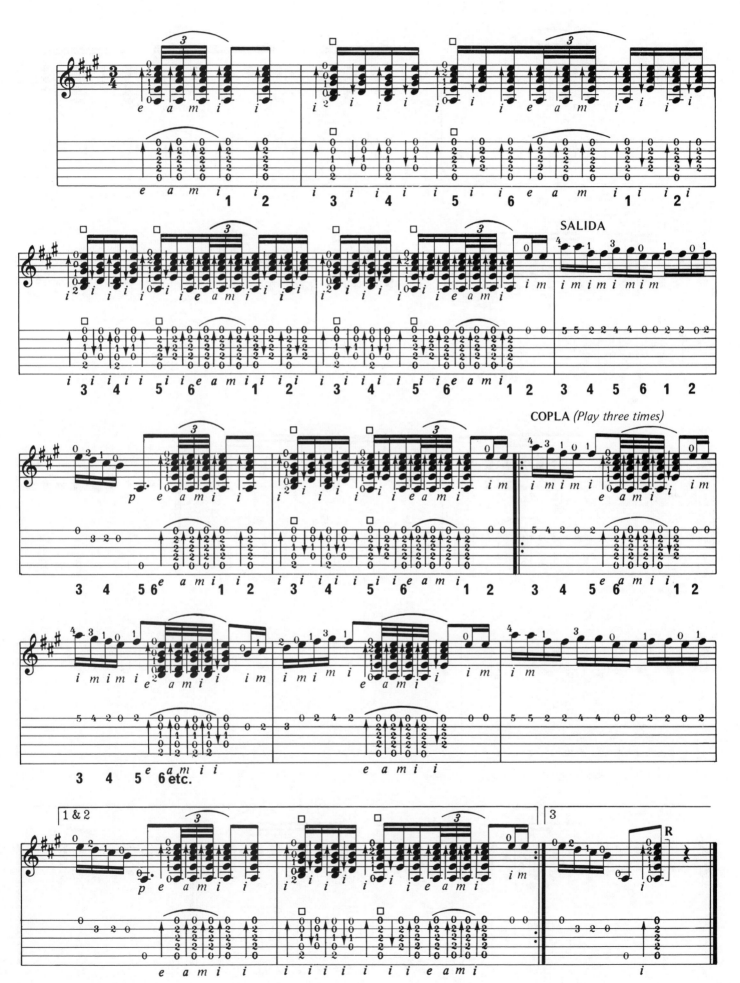

67

SEVILLANA 2

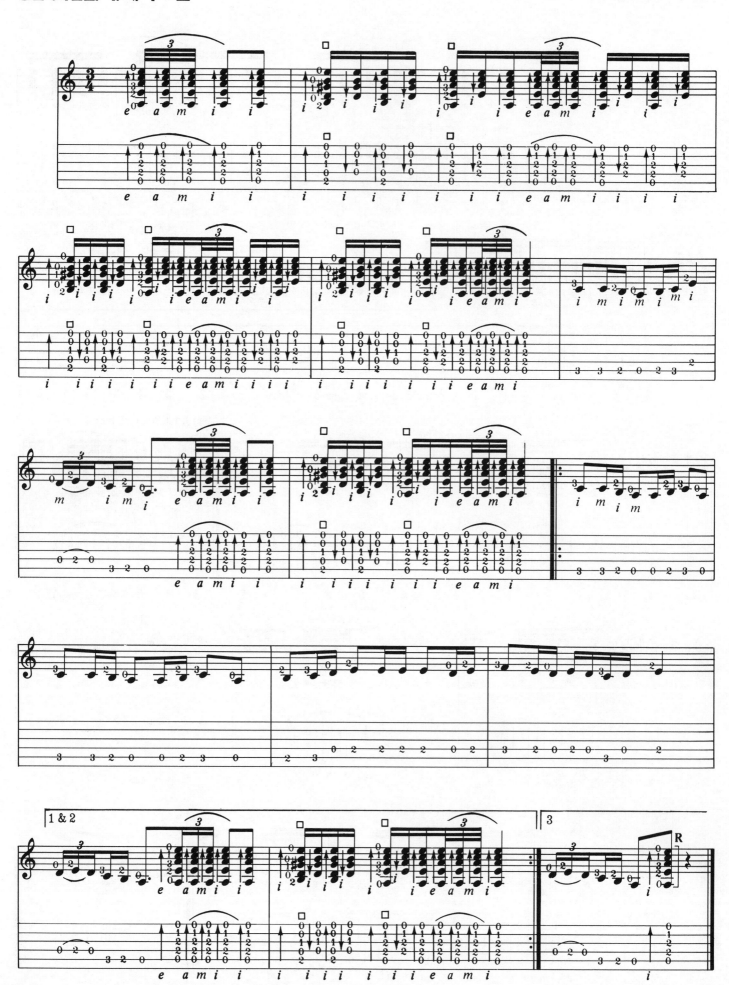

68

SEVILLANA 3

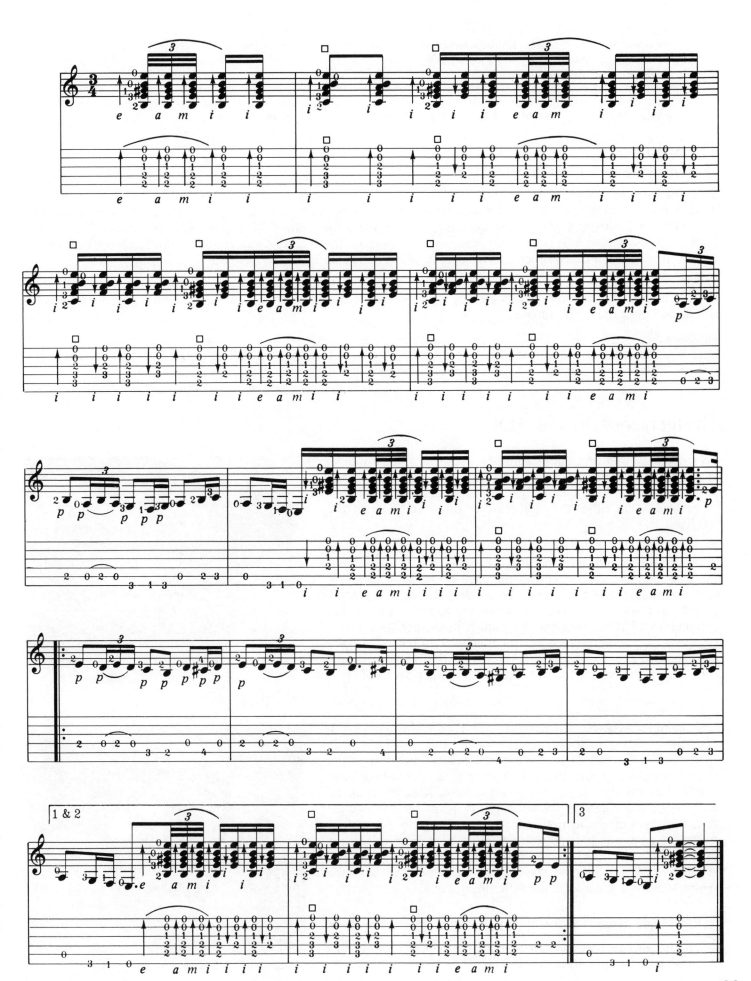

69

Counting the COMPÁS

The *compás* of Sevillanas can be counted all the way through in 6's. You need to understand how the melody fits in with the rhythm passages. It works out like this:

Beginning with count 1 on the first beat (which coincides with the index stroke of the first 4-stroke *rasgueo*) the introductory *rasgueo* passage can be counted in 6's, usually three times over. The *Salida,* and later the full melody, both begin on a count of 2 or 3, with the preceding count of 1 or 1 and 2 taken up by *rasgueo*. The ending of the *Salida* or of the full melody coincides with a count of 5. The following rhythm passage of *rasgueo* then begins from the count of 6 before starting through the 1 to 6 sequence again. After the third and final version of the melody there is usually an accented chord (here played with an index downstroke) on the count 6 to bring the music to a sudden stop. After a pause, the first beat of the next Sevillana starts again from the count of 1.

The solo

The three Sevillanas are in different keys.

Sevillana 1

Key: A major. The melody is played *picado* with alternating index and middle fingers of the right hand. It starts on the count of 2. Strongly played 5-stroke *rasgueos* punctuate the melody; the accent of each *rasgueo* falls on the final stroke with the index and coincides with the beat of the music. Contrast this with the 5-stroke *rasgueos* described in earlier lessons, which had the accent falling on the initial stroke with the little finger.

Sevillana 2

Key: A minor. The melody is again *picado*, but this time on the lower strings. Note that it starts on the count of 3 when you count the rhythm in 6's.

Sevillana 3

Here is an example of a Sevillana in the Phrygian mode based on E (or, as the Flamencos call it, *'por arriba'*). The melody is played with *apoyando* thumb-strokes on lower strings.

The technique of APAGADO

To stop the sound of a chord abruptly, as is heard, for instance, at the end of a Sevillana, the flamenco guitarist uses a technique called *apagado*, which means 'quenched' or 'silenced'. This can be performed by either the right hand or the little finger of the left hand, as follows:

Right hand APAGADO. Here, the right hand is brought down sharply onto the strings after striking them, in such a way that the base of the little finger and the edge of the palm instantly stop the vibration of the strings. To do this, the wrist is pushed smartly in towards the front surface of the guitar so that at the completion of the movement the hand is in the position shown in photo 10.1. The symbol used in this book to represent right hand *apagado* is a vertical bracket across the stave after the chord, with the letter R above it to indicate the right hand: **R**
]

10.1 Right hand apagado.

Left hand APAGADO. An alternative method of instantly stopping the vibration of the strings is to damp them with the little finger of the left hand, which is brought down straight across the strings at right-angles to them the instant after a chord has been sounded by the right hand. The position of the little finger at the end of the movement is shown in photo 10.2. The little finger needs to rest only momentarily across the strings to quench the sound. It does not press the strings against the fingerboard but just descends very quickly and lightly onto them. The symbol is a vertical bracket across the stave following the chord, with the figure 4 above it to indicate the little finger, i.e: 4
]

Right-hand *apagado* is the more powerful method of the two.

The little finger *apagado* can be repeated quickly, to produce a succession of abrupt ('staccato') chords.

10.2 Left hand apagado with little finger.

Elements of Flamenco 10   The rôle of the guitar

There are some people who regret the new status of the flamenco guitar as a solo concert instrument, fearing that it might have thereby lost touch with its earlier origins as an integral part of the *Cante*. It is true that the enormous interest today in the classical guitar has led many people to a serious appreciation of the flamenco instrument who may have only a very limited awareness of the musical context in which it developed. But one can take an optimistic view of this new popularity. It will encourage people outside Andalucía to look further than the guitar into the musical heritage, embodied especially in the *Cante*, from which the flamenco guitar draws so much of its strengths.

Flamenco is an improvised music deeply rooted in ancient traditions, which can give expression to the most personal and universal themes of hope and suffering. As a solo instrument, the flamenco guitar can do much more than just conjure up evocations of the *Cante* and *Baile*. It is ready to find a new validity on its own, able to give voice to all the most powerful emotions of Flamenco while retaining, and yet being partly distinct from, the inspiration of the *Cante*.

Today the art of solo playing can begin to acquire a new self-sufficiency and musicality, if only guitarists can start to advance beyond the sterile displays of speed and technical virtuosity into which so many good players have been led astray. Largely because of gramophone recording, standards of technique are far higher than ever before, but it is essential that these skills are seen as a means to an end rather than as an end in themselves.

The future possibilities reach out in many directions. The lure of pop music draws some players; yet one can be sure that it is only in so far as the flamenco guitar reaches deeper into the inspiration of the *Cante* and its early origins in Andalucía and cultures further south and eastward that its living tradition will grow further as a serious international presence in contemporary music.

The guitar in accompaniment

'Accompaniment' is not strong enough a term to describe the creative role of the guitarist in his collaboration with an accomplished singer. It is an equal partnership, a dialogue in which the performance of each artist complements the other so that the sum is greater than its parts. The ability to improvise and to be flexible in one's *toque* are among the special skills required if the guitarist is to complement his partner's performance to the full without appearing to compete or to intrude. For the *Cante*, the guitarist must have an extensive knowledge of the *coplas* and a deep identification with their *aire*, as well as a good ear for their harmonies, if he is to anticipate what the singer is going to do. The accompaniment of the *Baile* makes other demands as well, requiring an especially firm command of the *compás* and an instant responsiveness to the dancer's changes of tempo. To be able to accompany well is an essential aim if one is to become a flamenco guitarist in the fullest and truest sense.

Unfortunately for the student, the subtle arts of accompaniment for the *Cante* and *Baile* are more difficult to explore than the art of solo playing. To the concert-going public outside Spain they are still almost completely unknown and unappreciated.

Modern trends

Today there are signs that a second Golden Age of Flamenco is dawning, for there is rekindled interest in Flamenco in Spain and outside it. After a period of decline after the Civil War and until the 1960's, when the popularisation of showy, watered-down Flamenco in the theatre, in the tourist-traps of holiday resorts and on records became widespread, pure Flamenco is once again resurgent.

Today, Flamenco seems ready to resume its continuing process of evolution now that it has at last begun to recover in part from the disruption brought about by technological advance. Over the space of only a few decades this uniquely expressive and personal folk-music became subjected to an overwhelming onslaught of commercial pressures to sell its special magic to the enormous audience that could now be introduced to it. Inevitably the creative process came almost to a standstill and its deepest inspiration was all but lost sight of while only its more superficial and immediately attractive flamboyance could be marketed to a non-flamenco audience. Those commercial pressures will not abate, but at least there are now a growing number of people aware of what had nearly been destroyed, who seek to revive the creative force in Flamenco which was always part of its essence. The world outside Spain, awakening slowly to a recognition of the largely unfamiliar musical riches of the ancient cultures of southern Spain and North Africa, is readier now than ever before to be initiated into the authentic arts of Flamenco and to contribute to its future development.

In the guitar world in recent years there have been trends towards more complex syncopations and more 'modern' harmonies as well as numerous attempts, on record, to combine the flamenco guitar with other instruments. Nonetheless, *compás* and *aire*, those two indispensable ingredients, remain pre-eminent. Indeed there has been in the modern style a re-emphasis of the regular driving force of the *compás*, which had become diminished in importance in the days when the Fandango was almost all that survived of the flamenco *Cante* in public performance. Much earlier, there had been a rage for the Malagueñas of Juan Breva. Since the '60's, the Rumba has replaced the Fandango as the *cante* most popular with the non-flamenco audience. But there are encouraging signs that the audience for the more deeply flamenco *Cante* is growing rapidly. There is generally, as indeed there ought to be, a rediscovery of the *Cante* as the oldest and deepest expression of Flamenco.

LESSON 11   Trémolo

Trémolo is a technique for the solo guitar which gives the illusion of two instruments playing together. One, the treble voice, carries a flowing melodic line in which the impression of sustained sounds is created by very rapidly repeated notes, as on the mandolin. The other, the bass voice, plays a rhythmic accompaniment or counter-melody.

Development of right hand technique
Trémolo is introduced at this fairly early stage because it provides an excellent means of developing good right hand technique. It demands complete independence of movement of thumb and fingers and good control of each finger separately. You will need to practise it a great deal before you can begin to play it at anything near the sort of speed at which it sounds most effective, but if you can start to play it now, very slowly, in regular rhythm and with good independent control of the thumb and fingers you can be confident that your right hand is developing well.

The flamenco TRÉMOLO
The flamenco *trémolo* has five notes to a beat, with an initial thumbstroke on a bass note followed by four *tirando* strokes with the fingers on the treble: it is therefore written **p i a m i**. This has one more stroke than the *trémolo* for classical guitar which is **p a m i**, the technique used in Tárrega's famous *trémolo* study 'Recuerdos del Alhambra'.

 **CASSETTE: LESSON 11, TRÉMOLO**

The music which follows takes the form of a *falseta* for Soleares. It is played on the cassette at a slow speed so that you can hear each note of the *trémolo* clearly.

A Trémolo Falseta

Cejilla at 2nd fret

The left hand

For the first three bars of the *falseta*, the little finger of the left hand holds down A on the 1st string by stopping the string at the fifth fret, while fingers 1 and 2 move to stop notes on 5th, 4th and 3rd strings. In the fourth bar the left hand adopts a position of E major on the top four strings with the little finger stopping a G sharp at the fourth fret on the 1st string. The fifth bar introduces the new chord shape of G major, shown in diagram form and photo 11.1 on the right. The same chord shape may be fingered in different ways.

For the final three bars of the *falseta*, the left hand adopts in turn the chord positions of C major, F major and E major.

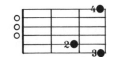

G major The chord diagram shows fingers 2 and 3 stopping the 5th and 6th strings and the photo shows an easier position using fingers 1 and 2 on these strings. Sometimes with the latter fingering, the 3rd finger stops the 1st string. The choice of fingering will depend on the musical context and the *toque*.

11.1 G major position (shown here with cejilla at 2nd fret).

The importance of the rhythm

Absolutely even rhythm is all-important in creating the illusion of an unbroken melody in the treble. The fingers must each strike distinctly, each with equal force and tone, and the spacing of the strokes with thumb and each finger must be regular.

Trémolo has been well called 'an arpeggio on a single string'. This way of viewing it will help you to concentrate on the even timing and spacing of the notes. Start *very slowly*, making sure that the intervals between **p i a m i** are all the same. The hand is relaxed and the fingers move primarily from the knuckles. The movements of the fingers are shown in 11.2(a) to (f).

You may be tempted to rush things in your eagerness to obtain the beautiful effect of the *trémolo* played rapidly. If you do, you are certain to develop bad habits which will cause unevenness of the rhythm. You will then find it much harder to make your *trémolo* smooth and flowing, but if you start right the speed will come naturally with practice.

The thumb in TRÉMOLO

The thumb plays *apoyando* or *tirando*, according to the effect desired. Where the bass notes are sounded in an ascending sequence of strings (e.g. 6th, 5th, 4th) the thumb, if playing *apoyando*, follows through to sound each one in turn without being lifted and swung back after each string has been sounded.

11.2 The flamenco trémolo. *a) Thumb strikes 6th string.*

b) Thumb apoyando *stroke arrested by 5th string.*

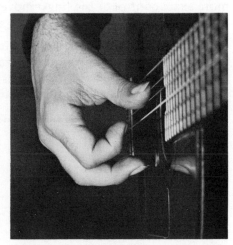

c) End of stroke with index.

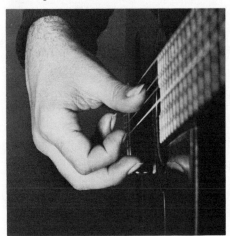

d) Third finger.

e) Middle finger.

f) Index again.

73

Besides playing the previous *falseta* as it is written, you will find it helpful, for practice purposes, to play it also with the 'classical' *trémolo* pattern **p a m i**. This will help you to ensure evenness of rhythm in the **a m i** sequence of strokes. In addition, again for practice only, you will help yourself to achieve correct movements of the fingers from the knuckles if you play both these *trémolo* patterns extremely slowly with each finger being swung to its fully flexed position so that it comes to rest against the base of the thumb at the end of its stroke (as was discussed in the introduction to *tirando*).

Two daily exercises for TRÉMOLO

Two exercises (not recorded on the cassette) are included here which will facilitate independent control of the four fingers. The first uses varied patterns of right hand fingering and must be played extremely slowly to start with.

Ex. 15

Ex. 16

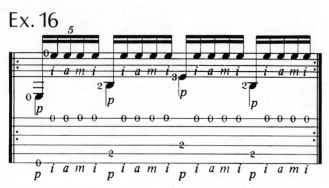

The second exercise is more difficult. Here the right hand fingers play *apoyando*, not *tirando*, and come to rest on the second string after they have struck the first. They are then kept in contact with the second string until each in turn is required for its next stroke. At any one moment, therefore, at least two of the three fingers, **a m** and **i**, should be resting on the 2nd string. Although hard initially, this exercise helps you develop strength as well as independence of the fingers.

TRÉMOLO on inner strings

So far, the *trémolo* notes have all been played on the 1st string. You should also practise these exercises playing the open 2nd and then the open 3rd string instead of the 1st. *Trémolo* on these inner strings is harder and requires more exact control of the finger movements.

Checking the regularity

Once you begin to play *trémolo* with some facility and are beginning to increase your speed gradually, a tape-recording of your playing, played back at half the tape-speed at which you recorded it, will give you valuable insights into any minor irregularities of rhythm and emphasis. If your rhythm is even enough to pass this very critical test you are well on the road to acquiring a fine *trémolo*.

LESSON 12   Bulerías (i)

The rapid impetus and bouncing pulse of the Bulerías make this the most exciting *toque* in Flamenco. It can be the greatest challenge to the guitarist and the most brilliant showpiece for his virtuosity. You may, therefore, be surprised to find it introduced at so early a stage in the book. The reasons are twofold.

The first has to do with the nature of Bulerías and its role in Flamenco today. It is a *toque* of central importance, with an enormous range and variety of expression possible within it. At its heart is a powerfully rhythmic motor, a driving force which is part of the very essence of Flamenco. The energy of this steady pulsation is something you should begin to generate as early as possible in your playing and to recognise in your listening.

The second, and closely related, reason has to do with your whole approach to the flamenco guitar. It is emphasised again and again throughout this book that the excitement of flamenco rhythm does not depend primarily on speed but on the basic pulsation and accentuation of the *compás*. By learning to play Bulerías very slowly at this stage, you will be able to concentrate on bringing out the feeling of its steady pulse and its accents, both in the *rasgueo* and the *falsetas*. The speed can be left to come of its own good time. This way you will learn it much more effectively than if you rush ahead too fast and lose the regular pacing of the rhythm.

Historical development

The word 'Bulería' seems likely to be a *gitano* derivation from *burlería* which means tom-foolery or ridicule. There are various theories about how the *toque* evolved. It appears to be a fairly recent development of the *Cante Gitano*, perhaps hardly more than a century old. Styles have changed and are continuing to do so.

Bulerías now constitute a *toque*, still particularly associated with the *gitanos*, which has great flexibility. It has well been called 'omnivorous', since such a wide variety of themes, including pop songs and even, in regrettable taste, some non-Spanish tunes, have been set to its *compás*. Many dances, especially Soleares and Alegrías but sometimes even other *toques*, are commonly brought to a dramatic final climax by finishing with Bulerias.

The *compás* shows it to be very closely related to Soleares. Possibly it started with the faster music *(remates)* with which *gitano* singers liked to end Soleares. El Loco Mateo ('Mad Matthew') of Jerez is known to have done this about 1870.

The earlier styles of Bulerías are quite slow in pace and are called *Bulerías al Golpe*, because of their marked rhythm with strongly emphasised accents. Diego del Gastor (d.1973) was a magnificent player for these older *cantes*, which deserve to be far more widely known and performed. They are closer in *aire* to such intermediate forms as the *Soleá por Bulerías* than to the much faster styles of recent times. The *aire* can be passionate and serious or even tragic, in contrast to the festive gaiety or uproarious frivolity and ecstatic abandon which prevail in the faster Bulerías.

The faster Bulerías, known as *Bulerías Ligadas* because of their more flowing and less abrupt rhythm, have become very popular as cheerful and often humorous songs, as the accompaniment for festive dances and as guitar solos of thrilling virtuosity.

Already the guitar style in Bulerías has moved on a long way, even in comparison with styles of, say, ten years ago. Within the same overall *compás*, the *aire* has altered with the introduction of new *rasgueos*, more complex syncopation and *contratiempo* and new harmonies derived from jazz-influenced popular music.

The COMPÁS of Bulerías

The basic *compás* of Bulerías follows the same pattern as a Soleares. It is made up of sequences of 12 beats with accents on beats 3, 6, 8, 10 and 12. i.e.:

$$1 \quad 2 \quad \overset{>}{3} \quad 4 \quad 5 \quad \overset{>}{6} \quad 7 \quad \overset{>}{8} \quad 9 \quad \overset{>}{10} \quad 11 \quad \overset{>}{12}$$

Besides its faster pace, other components of the rhythm give the Bulerías its own special character. These will be stated briefly now, but the principles described can only begin to make much sense when you have studied the musical illustrations in this lesson and Lessons 13 and 15.

Much of the apparent complexity of Bulerías stems from the fact that within the overall *compás* in 12's there are other inner-rhythms best counted in 6's, as well as subtle syncopations and variations of accentuation. The correct timing of *falsetas* is especially important.

The beginnings of FALSETAS

Many *falsetas* for Bulerías start (like those in Soleares) on the count of 1. But there are many others that begin on the earlier count of 12, after a *rasgueo* passage with its final accent on 10. Some *falsetas* start earlier still on the count of 11 or even occasionally on 10.

The duration and endings of FALSETAS

Falsetas vary in length. The melodic phrases of which they are composed can be counted within multiples of 6 beats. The melody may span an odd or even number of sequences of 6 beats, but the overall framework of the 12-beat *compás* has to be preserved. How is this done?

The answer lies in the number of beats played with *rasgueo* at the end of the *falseta*. If we are counting in sequences of 1 to 6, the last note of the *falseta* usually falls on the count of 4. Where the *falseta* has an uneven number of 6's, there will be 8 beats to be completed before the next 12-beat *compás* begins. These are taken up by a passage of *rasgueo*. Where the *falseta* has, on the other hand, an even number of 6's, the final note falls on the beat equivalent to 10 when we count in 12's. There are then only 2 beats to be completed before the next 12-beat *compás*.

So, if the *falseta* has an uneven multiple of 6's, it will require the longer type of *rasgueo* ending.

Quite often the *falseta* is composed of short phrases (sometimes repeated) followed by a longer phrase. Similar principles apply. If any of the phrases fall within an uneven multiple of 6's — as, for example when the *falseta* begins with a phrase starting on 12 and ending on the first count of 6 — then the longer type of *rasgueo* 'fill-in' passage is needed before the next phrase starts on 12. In this way the 12-beat *compás* is preserved.

The rhythm of the PALMAS

The hand-clapping *(palmas)* in Bulerías provides the essential clue to understanding how the 12-beat *compás* with accents on beats 3, 6, 8, 10, 12 can also be counted as two identical 6-beat sequences. When we count in 6's, the handclaps occur on beats 1, 2 and 4, 5 like this:

```
      *    *       *    *       *    *       *    *
      1    2    3    4    5    6    1    2    3    4    5    6
```

The same rhythm is heard at times in *golpes* on the guitar and may be emphasised also in some types of *rasgueo* and *falsetas*.

You can get the feeling of this by practising the hand-claps (see p. 85 for details of the correct flamenco technique) while you count aloud in 6's. Clap your hands twice over towards your left side on counts 1 and 2 and twice over towards your right on counts 4 and 5. This way you will quickly feel the 'swing' of the rhythm.

Putting the two kinds of rhythm, in 12's and 6's, together and adding the bar-lines from the musical notation, we now have:

Palmas		*	*		*	*		*	*		*	*	
Count in 12's	1	2	3	4	5	6	7	8	9	10	11	12	
Count in 6's	1	2	3	4	5	6	1	2	3	4	5	6	

Ending Bulerías

As in Soleares and Alegrías, Bulerías ends with its final chord being played on a count of 10.

CONTRATIEMPO

The *compás* in 12's and the inner-rhythm in 6's together provide the rhythmic basis for Bulerías. When you first hear a *cuadro* (flamenco troupe) performing Bulerías it may sound much more complicated than this because further syncopations can be introduced by the guitarist in *rasgueos* and *falsetas*, and by the hand-clapping and the dancer's *taconeo* (heel-work). We have shown only the beats above, but other accents can be added on the intervening half-beats. Once you have understood the essential form of the *compás*, however, you will hear it emerge clearly, with all these possible additional elements fitting within its basic pattern.

Musical notation and tonality

The Bulerías in this book are written in a fast 3/4 time. 3/8 would be more appropriate to the speed, but 3/4 allows greater clarity of symbols.

The music of the Bulerías in Lessons 12, 13 and 15 is played in the *'por medio'* position, that is in the Phrygian mode based on A. For the most part the chords are similar to those you have already met in Seguiriyas.

Bulerías may also be played in other keys, both major and minor, as well as in the Phrygian mode based on E or even (a recent innovation) on F♯ as in Tarantas.

The first solo Bulerías

The first example of Bulerías *(opposite)* is played fairly slowly on the cassette recording so that you can hear the *compás* clearly. When you play the solo you will find it best to study the music in sections of one or two *compases*

CASSETTE: LESSON 12, FIRST BULERÍAS

at a time. Master the rhythm of each of them before you move on to the next. The solo begins with five *compases* of *rasgueo* rhythm. These are separately numbered in the music.

COMPÁS 1

Compás 1 consists entirely of index finger downstrokes on the chord of A major with a *ligado* 'hammer-on' from A to B♭ on the 3rd string added on the half-beats. The *compás* demonstrates the accents on beats 3, 6, 8, 10 and 12 and you should bring these out clearly by giving extra emphasis to the downstrokes on these beats. In addition, if you can, play a *golpe* to coincide with each accented downstroke. The timing must be very exact if the *golpe* is to sound simultaneously with a crisp impact from the index downstroke. If you are not yet confident about combining a *golpe* with the downstroke, leave it out to start with so that you can concentrate on getting the feel of the rhythm with the index strokes.

COMPÁS 2

The 3, 6, 8, 10, 12 accentuation continues here but we now have index upstrokes on the half-beats after 7 and 8 and then a 5-stroke *rasgueo* starting on beat 9 with its accent on beat 10. The count of 10 coincides with the final index upstroke of the *rasgueo*.

Together, *compases* 1 and 2 provide a typical introduction to a Bulerías. They illustrate very clearly how much of the exciting pulse of the music can be generated just by good right hand control and a feeling for the bounce of the rhythm, using only a single chord and single strokes. Once you have got this motor drive inside you and into your right hand, the rest of Bulerías can follow naturally and logically for you.

COMPÁS 3

Here a chord change to a B♭ chord (with E on the open 1st string) coincides with the marked accent on beat 3 and the chord change back to A coincides with the beat on 7. 2 beats of *golpe* on 4 and 5 must be exactly timed. The ending of the *compás* is similar to the previous one. (In the musical notation, the B♭ chord on beat 3 is written as a crotchet tied to a minim in the second bar. The minim is not played separately but is written in to indicate that the sound of the chord is allowed to sustain from beat 3 until just before beat 6. The *cifra* also shows the actual right hand strokes.) This *compás* can be used a lot in Bulerías as a *rasgueo* passage which maintains the continuity of the rhythm. *Compases* 5 and 12 are the same one again. You could start Bulerías with it, either from the count of 1 (as in Bulerías No. 3, to follow) or from the upstroke on the previous count of 12.

COMPÁS 4

This is another variant of the basic 3, 6, 8, 10, 12 pattern, with upstrokes on the half-beats after beats 3 and 4. There are two new chords, both fingered in the musical notation. The first is a version of B♭ with F on the 1st string, and the second is derived from C7 with an added D on the 2nd string.

First Bulerías

Cejilla at 3rd fret

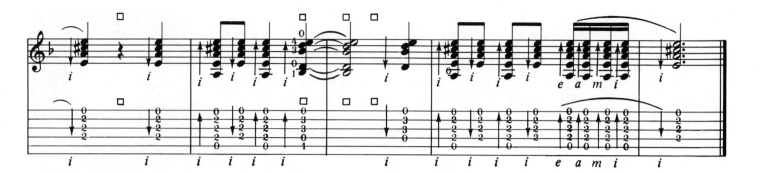

The FALSETA *(opposite page)*

This traditional *falseta* is typical of many in Bulerías which start on a count of 12. Two melodic phrases, each in turn repeated once, make up the first part of the *falseta*. They are played *picado* with **i** and **m**. Remember to observe the rule about always alternating the fingers in *picado*.

After the first beat of the melody on the count 12, each *picado* phrase occupies another 6 beats. The following *rasgueo* sequence therefore has to last 5 more beats to complete the *compás* before the next phrase starts, again on the count of 12. In this way the recurring pattern of 12-beat *compases* is preserved throughout the first part of the *falseta*.

Like many *falsetas*, this one has two parts, allowing the performer a choice of second part to follow the first. One could think of it as two *falsetas*, except that the first part (the *picado* phrases) all relate to just one chord (A7 with G on the open 3rd string) and would sound incomplete if played on their own. The second part played here (which could also be used as a brief *falseta* on its own or as an ending to another *falseta*) also starts on the count of 12. It then occupies only 1½ *compases* (i.e. 3 x 6's), so that the concluding *rasgueo* again has to be of the longer kind for this part of the *falseta* (and the *falseta* as a whole) to conform to the pattern of 12-beat *compases*.

The melody section of the second part of the *falseta* introduces the use of thumb upstrokes, an *alzapúa* technique which will be described below.

The left hand also deserves comment. Fingers 4 and 3 are held down on the 2nd and 3rd strings, respectively, throughout the second part of the *falseta*. Fingers 2 and 1 move to stop notes on the 5th string. Notice how the 2nd finger is used to stop the C♯ at the fourth fret on the 5th string, as shown in 12.1 overleaf.

ALZAPÚA

The name *alzapúa* (from *alzar* = 'lift' or 'raise' and *púa* = 'point' or 'plectrum') comes from the use of upstrokes with the thumb in this very flamenco technique, which imparts a strongly rhythmic and syncopated pulsation to melodic passages.

In its most typical form today, *alzapúa* consists of a rapidly repeated pattern of three types of stroke with the right hand thumb. The thumb-strokes are played in the following order:

1. First, the thumb plays a downstroke chord across the strings, starting from a well-defined note as the lowest note of the chord that is sounded. This note belongs to the melody and is the most important part of the chord, whose exact extent onto higher strings is therefore not crucial. A *golpe* is often played to coincide with the thumb-stroke. For example:

2. Next, the thumb plays a strong upstroke on the same chord, hitting across the strings with the edge of the nail. It is the emphasis on this upstroke which gives the rhythm its characteristic syncopation and urgency. The exact extent of the upstroke does not have to be very clearly defined because it is essentially part of the rhythm, not the melody.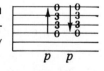

3. Thirdly, the thumb plays a single melody note with a firm *apoyando* stroke on a bass string. This string is either the same string as the one the next downstroke of the thumb starts from or, commonly, it is the next one lower. In the latter case the thumb swings on to sound the next downstroke chord on its follow-through after striking the single note.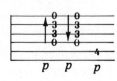

The right hand is in the 'thumb' position as shown in Lesson 2. The thumb swings from its joint at the wrist. The left hand finger movements are based on chord positions; these are held down by some fingers while other fingers are kept on the move stopping the melody notes./*continued overleaf*

ALZAPÚA *(continued)*

The example of this technique in the preceding Bulerías is a good way of making one's first acquaintance with *alzapúa* thumbstrokes, because they are played fairly slowly here. Each of the three strokes with the thumb (down-, up-, and single note *apoyando*) occurs at half-beat intervals of time. In other *toques* and elsewhere in Bulerías the three together are often written as a triplet, occurring within the duration of a single beat. Commonly, too, passages of *alzapúa* are taken at a faster tempo than the rest of the piece in which they occur, in order to heighten their exciting effect.

Alzapúa can be used in various *toques*. Although developed in recent years as a virtuoso technique of great brilliance, its origins are probably ancient, for similar techniques are heard in music for the Islamic *'ud*, a southern cousin and ancestor of the guitar.

12.1 2nd finger stopping C sharp.

The use of thumb upstrokes was formerly common practice in Flamenco, not only in *rasgueo* but also in the playing of single note runs, the player using his thumbnail like a plectrum. Nowadays this is nearly obsolete for single note passages, though it is still sometimes to be heard, particularly in the flamenco guitar tradition of Morón de la Frontera.

LESSON 13   Bulerías (ii)

In this lesson there are two more sequences of Bulerías to illustrate the *compás*. Each of them introduces, in addition, a new *rasgueo* technique.

Second Bulerías

Whereas the First Bulerías showed clearly the 3, 6, 8, 10, 12 pattern of accents in the *compás* the Second Bulerías highlights also the other main type of rhythm, the accents on beats 1, 2 and 4, 5 when we count the *compás* in 6's.

In the music the counting of the *compás* is shown in 12's. Where the accents of the rhythm relate to the count of 6's, therefore, we find them occurring on counts 1, 2, 4, 5, 7, 8 and 10, 11.

COMPÁS 1 demands very exact control of the timing and precise coordination of the *rasgueo* and left hand *apagado* with the little finger. Only beats 1, 2, 4, 5, 7, 10 and 11 are sounded, the sound of each chord being cut off crisply by the *apagado*. The *rasgueo* is a variation from the usual 4-stroke *rasgueo*. The normal sequence of **e a m i** strokes has been divided into two component parts, **e-a-m** and **i**, in order to give a very abrupt, staccato sound.

The right hand fingers are first flexed into the palm so that the fingernails do actually press into the palm. The thumb rests lightly on the 6th string. For the first part of the *rasgueo* the fingers **e, a, m** are flicked out in rapid sequence against the resistance provided by the ball and base of the thumb, so that the stroke with the middle finger coincides with beat 1. The preceding strokes with **e** and **a** hit the strings an instant before the beat.

Immediately after the middle finger has made its stroke, the sound of the chord is instantly silenced by a light *apagado* with the little finger of the left hand (see photo 13.1 for the position of the fingers at this point).

The right index finger, which until this time has remained pressed against the base of the thumb, is then flicked out against the resistance of the thumb to give a very crisp downstroke which coincides with beat 2. Beat 3 is silent.

The same thing is repeated on beats 4 and 5, with 6 again silent. For the beat on the count of 7, only three fingers, **e, a** and **m,** are flicked out. The **e** and **a** strokes again precede the beat by fractions of a second. Beats 8 and 9 are silent and 10 and 11 are sounded in the same way as beats 1 and 2 or 4 and 5. Each time the sound is silenced by the *apagados*. *Golpes* on beats 2, 5, 8 and 11 are optional.

COMPÁS 2: here beats 1, 2, 4, 5 and 11 are sounded by *golpes* alone. On beat 12 there is a chord of A7, with G at the 3rd fret on the 1st string. This G is 'pulled off' by the 3rd finger to sound the E of the open 1st string on the half-beat which follows 12.

COMPÁS 3 again has *golpes* on beats 1, 2 and 4, 5. The *ligado* on beat 3 needs precise timing. It is a 'pull-off' from F to E on the first string.

13.1 *Left hand* apagado *after* rasgueo *with* **e a** *and* **m** *in the Second Bulerías, as described in the text.*

As mentioned previously, the 'ties' joining chords in the musical notation indicate the duration of their sound. Only the first chord in each tied pair is actually struck.

COMPÁS 4 is similar to the type of 'fill-in' *compás* which was repeated in the First Bulerías. Note how the Bulerías again, as in all sequences of this *toque*, ends with the last chord being struck on the count of 10. The sound of this chord is sustained here, but often it is cut short abruptly after the beat by use of *apagado*.

🔲 **CASSETTE: LESSON 13, SECOND BULERÍAS**

Second Bulerías

Cejilla at 3rd fret

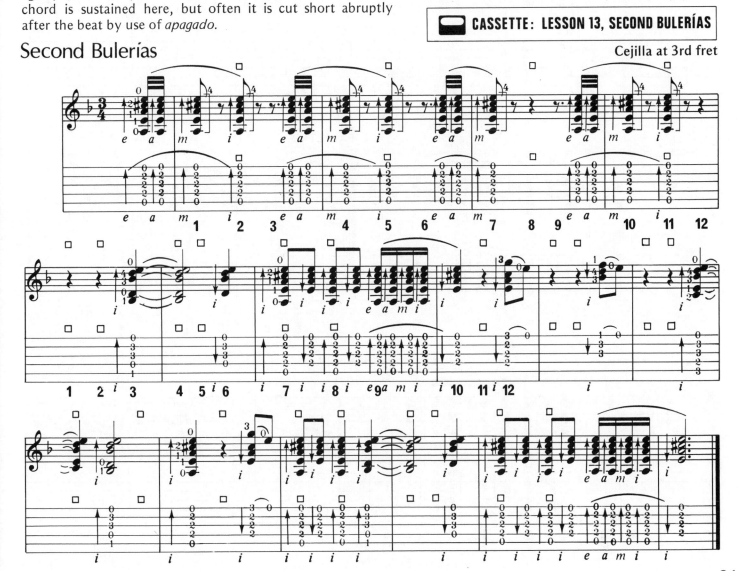

Third Bulerías

This sequence of Bulerías includes two more traditional *falsetas* and introduces an exciting technique for the right hand, the 3-stroke, triplet *rasgueo*.

The first FALSETA

The first *falseta* is an example of a *falseta* which starts on the count of 1. It provides a good example of the old saying that it is the exception that proves the rule, since at first sight it does not seem to obey the rule that all *falsetas* should fit within a multiple of 12 beats. The first melodic phrase fits within an even multiple of 6's and this is followed by what we have earlier referred to as the longer type of *rasgueo* ending, adding another 6 beats (from B to C in the music, played on the A7 chord with open 3rd string introduced in the First Bulerías). The longer ending seems wrong here and *fuera de compás*. But because the whole passage (from A to C) is repeated, the first part of the *falseta*, consisting of 6 x 6 beats, does actually fit into 12's and is *a compás*. You can see this clearly if you count the repeat on from 6 at C the first time, as shown in the lower line of numbers in the music.

In the ending phrase which follows the repeated section, study carefully the way the *ligado* is performed in the bar marked D to give a syncopated finish to the *falseta*.

 CASSETTE: THIRD BULERÍAS

Cejilla at 3rd fret

Third Bulerías

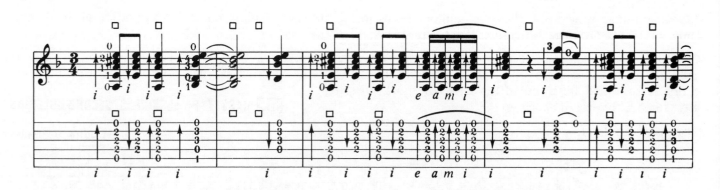

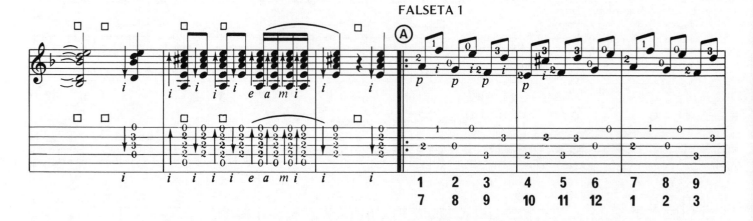

FALSETA 1

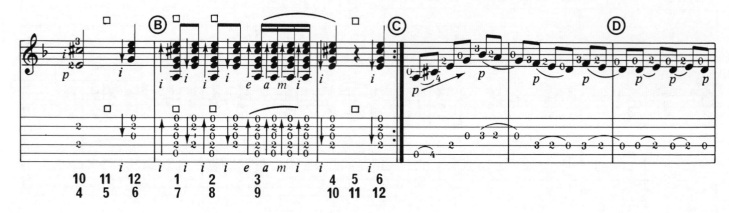

The second FALSETA

The second *falseta* starts on the count of 12. The first part is the same as a well-known traditional *falseta* for Seguiriyas and it illustrates the close relationship that exists between these two groups of *toques* (as discussed in more detail on p.145). The second part of the *falseta* shows another example of upstrokes with the thumb.

The 3-stroke triplet *rasgueo* is played in the final *compás*. A detailed description of this technique follows overleaf, on p.84. The ending of the solo has been played slowly and recorded separately on the cassette so that you can hear the accents and rhythm of this new *rasgueo* clearly.

CASSETTE: THIRD BULERÍAS, FINAL COMPÁS PLAYED SLOWLY

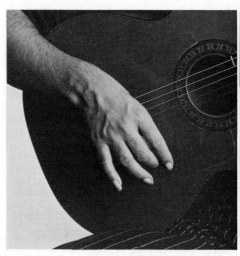

13.2 The triplet rasgueo. *(a) Starting position.*   *(b) Thumb strikes upwards.*   *(c) Completion of thumb upstroke.*

(d) Downstroke with middle finger.   *(e) Downstroke with thumb.*   *(f) Completion of thumb downstroke.*

The triplet RASGUEO

The final *compás* of the Third Bulerías introduces the technique of the 3-stroke triplet *rasgueo* with thumb and middle finger. Its powerful rhythmic effect has made it widely popular among guitarists today.

The three strokes of the *rasgueo* may be repeated rapidly in succession to give a prolonged roll. They should each be clearly audible and evenly spaced in time:

1.   First, the *thumb* plays a strong *upstroke* across all the strings to be included in a chord (here initially a chord of F major).

2.   Next, the *middle finger* makes a *downstroke* across the strings.

3.   Then the *thumb* plays a *downstroke* across the strings.

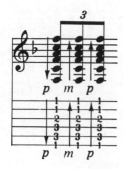

The next stroke after (3) is always a strong *thumb upstroke* across the strings. This is either the start of another 3-stroke *rasgueo* (i.e. (1) above) or it is a concluding stroke, which may be followed by further index strokes or may be the final chord of a phrase or section of the piece.

The accents of the *rasgueo* always fall on the upstrokes with the thumb. Thus in the Third Bulerías, the *rasgueo* is written in triplets, indicating that all three strokes fall within the duration of one beat of the *compás*. The following upstroke with the thumb coincides with the next beat.

When the *rasgueo* is played at a faster speed elsewhere (and it may be very rapid) each triplet often occupies the duration of one half-beat.

84

The power of the *rasgueo* comes from a combination of movement of thumb and middle finger together with movement of the whole hand from the wrist. The hand starts from a position similar to the 'thumb' position. It is important that the wrist should be arched enough to bring the line of the thumb upstroke towards a line at right-angles across the strings. The downstroke with the midde finger is a flick-like uncurling of the finger (as in the usual downstroke with the index). It does not quite touch the palm at its starting position. The downstroke with the thumb is a firm sweep across the strings.

To bring thumb and middle finger into correct positions for their strokes the hand is swung freely from a very relaxed wrist. There is a to-and-fro movement of the wrist as well as a very slight amount of clockwise rotation (as seen from your viewpoint as you play).

Here is another example of the many uses of the three-stroke *rasgueo*, this time to the *compás* of Soleares. Play it again and again until you have the rhythm exactly right:

CASSETTE: A COMPÁS OF SOLEARES WITH TRIPLET RASGUEOS

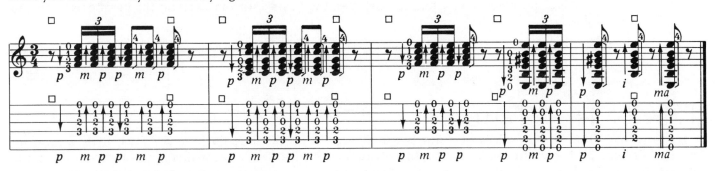

Elements of Flamenco 11   Palmas

The playing of *palmas* (handclaps) in Flamenco demands very considerable skill and knowledge of *compás* if it is to be performed well. The newcomer to Flamenco often believes, mistakenly, that *palmas* (or the vocal encouragement of the *jaleo*) demand only indiscriminate enthusiasm, but this is very far from being the case.

The photos below show the two basic techniques, *palmas sordas* and *palmas fuertes*, described overleaf.

13.3   **PALMAS SORDAS**   13.4   **PALMAS FUERTES**

PALMAS SORDAS

Palmas sordas (literally 'deaf' handclaps) are played with the fingers flexed and the hands loosely cupped. The sound is 'hollow' and much less penetrating compared to the much louder and sharper sound of *palmas fuertes*. A flamenco singer will play *palmas sordas* to emphasise the *compás* when he is accompanied by a guitarist, or they may be used by a *cuadro* in quieter passages of accompaniment to dancing or singing.

PALMAS FUERTES

Palmas fuertes ('strong' handclaps) are played with the fingers extended. The palmar surfaces of the first three fingers of the right hand are clapped against the slightly cupped palm of the left to produce, with practice, a powerful and abrupt sound.

You will need to listen to many records or live performances to begin to understand the proper use of *palmas* in the different *toques*. Often a syncopated counter-rhythm *(contratiempo)* is played by clapping on the half-beats. An excitingly rapid alternation of claps can be played by the performers, one clapping on the beat, the other on the intervening half-beats. To acquire a feeling for the *contratiempo* you can practise by beating time on the beat with your foot, making each clap sound exactly midway between the beats with the foot, on the half-beats. You can build up the speed slowly.

LESSON 14   Farruca

People who hail from the provinces of Asturias and Galicia in northern Spain have been called *farrucos*. The flamenco Farruca probably arose in Cádiz by the adaptation of melodies brought there by travellers from these northern regions. Although a *cante* is still sometimes performed, the Farruca today exists almost entirely as a dance-form and as music for the guitar. It is not one of the most profound *toques* but it can make an attractive guitar solo. The chords are played on the guitar in the key positions of A minor, or occasionally other minor keys (e.g. D minor). There may also be brief passages in the Phrygian mode.

The COMPÁS and AIRE

The rhythm is a regular 4/4 (i.e. with 4 beats to each bar or 'measure') and the character of the music is virile and emphatic. Changes in tempo follow the variations of the *baile*, a man's dance which is dramatic and strongly masculine, with some allusions to the *corrida* in its postures and movements.

The A minor key and regular 4/4 rhythm make the Farruca one of the least complicated *toques* for the guitarist but it is important to bring out the strong character of the music and not to let it become dull or merely prettified. At its best the Farruca can be very flamenco, with a powerful propulsion in the rhythm and a poignant melancholy, tinged sometimes with a faintly oriental quality in the lyrical melodies.

The solo

The solo which follows is the longest so far in the book, in order to show the range of techniques used in traditional *falsetas*. The rhythm is a marked 4/4 but there is also often a feeling of 2/4 to it, with emphasis on the first and third beats of each 4-beat bar. At times the music accelerates to a dramatic climax but at others, as in the *trémolo falseta*, it slows to a more lyrical, flowing melody. Near the end, the music accelerates to a faster tempo, with a traditional passage in A major being followed by a rapid finale in A minor. This faster ending again mirrors the dance and might not always be appropriate in other guitar solos.

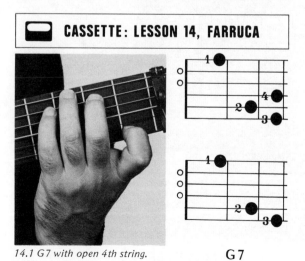

CASSETTE: LESSON 14, FARRUCA

14.1 G7 with open 4th string.   G7

The *falsetas* use techniques already described, including *picado*, thumb *apoyando*, octaves and *trémolo*. The *rasgueo* introduction starts with the traditional chord sequence of E7 (with B, C♯, D, B on the second string) A minor and D minor (see photos 14.2, 14.3 and 14.4 opposite). Later sequences show examples of typical flamenco syncopations which will need careful attention to the rhythm of the *golpes*, down- and upstrokes and left hand *apagados*.

Included among the new chord shapes for the left hand which you will meet in this solo are two versions of G7 (the dominant seventh in the key of C). In the first of these, shown in the upper of the two chord diagrams on the left, the fourth finger stops an F on the 4th string at the third fret. In the later version, played at the start of the *trémolo falseta* and shown in the photo 14.1, the 4th string is open.

14.2 E7 chord position. 3rd finger poised over 2nd fret.

14.3 E7 with C sharp stopped by 3rd finger.

14.4 E7 with 3rd and 4th fingers stopping 2nd string.

FARRUCA

Cejilla at 2nd Fret

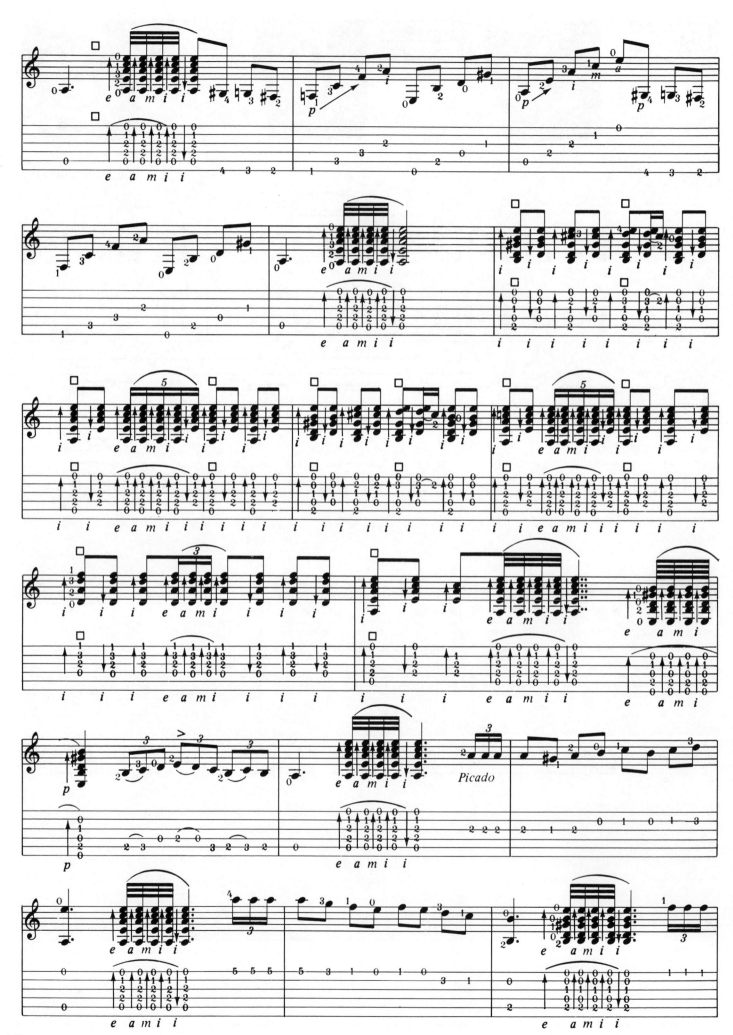

88

89

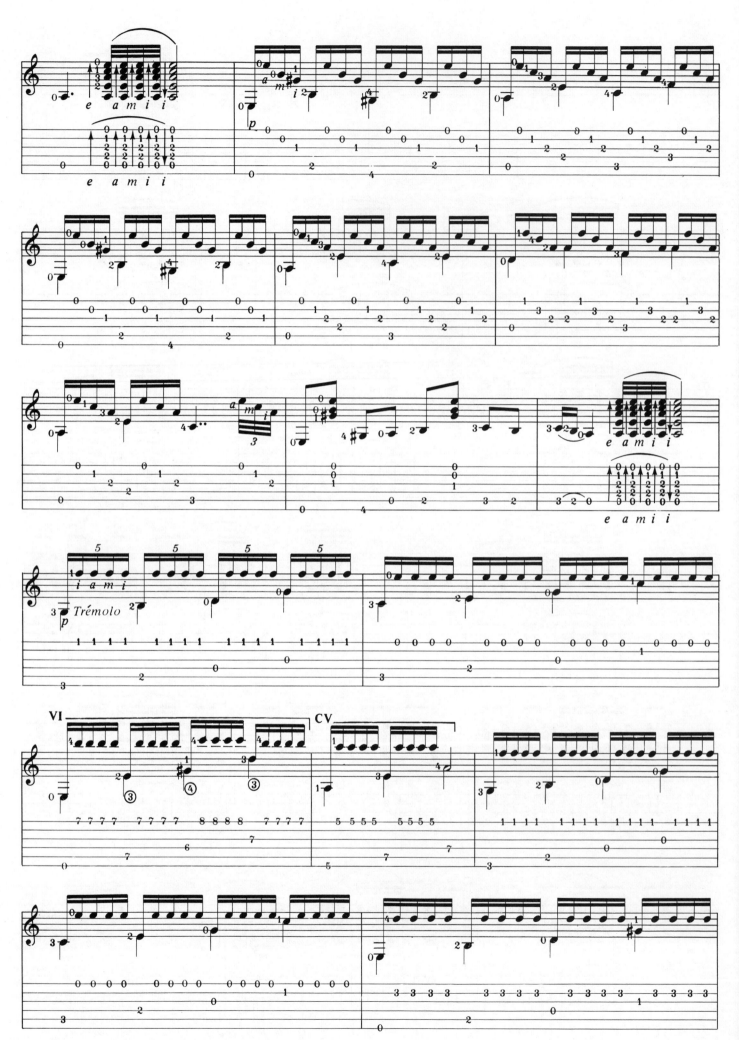

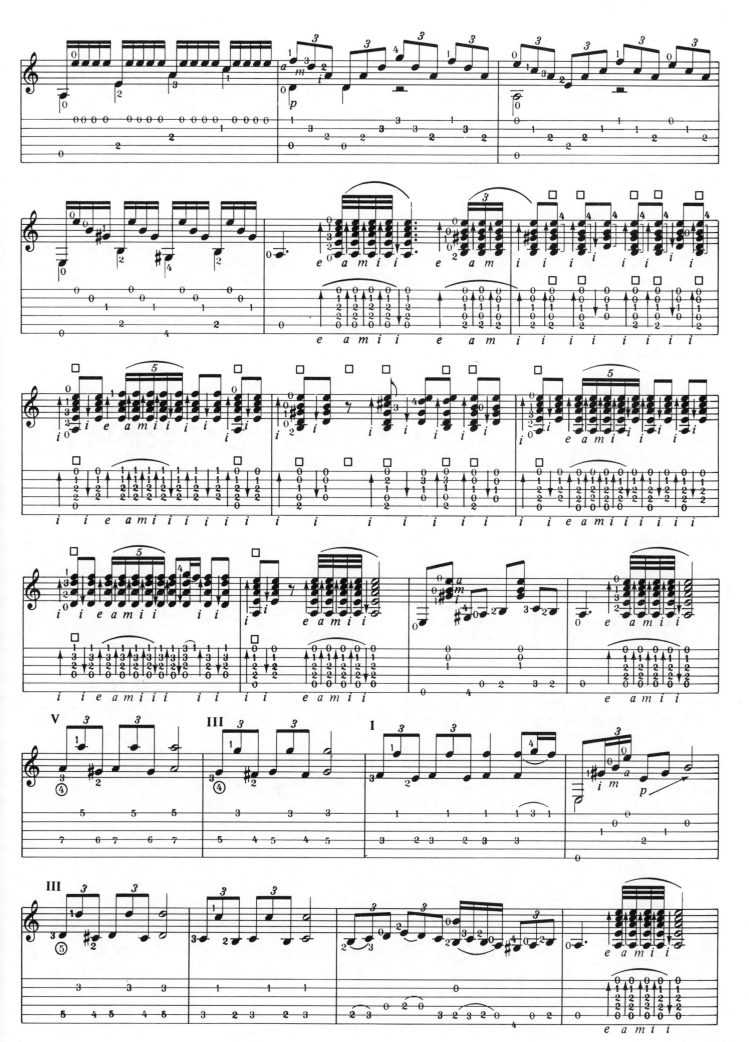

LESSON 15   Bulerías (iii)

The longer solo Bulerías which follows contains four more traditional *falsetas* together with further types of *rasgueo compás*. These show the 3, 6, 8, 10, 12 pattern as well as, in some places, the 1, 2, 4, 5 pattern of accents or *golpes* relating to the count in 6's. The first two *falsetas* are played with the thumb (including thumb upstrokes in the first) and the third and fourth are mainly *picado.* They start either on the count of 12 (*falsetas* 1, 3 and 4) or on the count of 1 (*falseta* 2). The techniques used have been described earlier, but two

▭ CASSETTE, SIDE TWO: LESSON 15, FOURTH BULERÍAS

passages of *rasgueo* need further explanation, as follows:

The two introductory *compases* (from A to B in the notation) have the same rhythmic form as the introduction to the First Bulerías. The right hand strokes, however, are not the same since two different kinds of downstroke replace the simpler index downstrokes of the First Bulerías. They illustrate techniques widely used in present-day Flamenco.

(i) **Downstrokes made by middle and ring fingers simultaneously** (represented by the symbol ↑ma) are played on beats 1, 2, 4, 5, 7, 9, 11 in the first *compás* and beats 1, 2, 4, 5 in the second. Both fingers move together as a unit from the knuckles, as shown in photo 15.1. The extra weight behind the stroke gives it a powerful, decisive sound.

15.1 Downstroke with m *and* a *together. (a) Starting position.*

(b) End of stroke.

(ii) **Flicked-out index downstrokes** (combined with *golpes*) occur on other beats (3, 6, 8, 10, 12 in the first *compás* and 3, 6, 7 and 8 in the second). In previous downstrokes with the index, the finger has not actually touched the flesh at the base of the thumb. Here, however, the index stroke starts from the position shown in photo 15.2 so that it is flicked strongly against the resistance provided by the thumb to give a more powerful, faster stroke.

You will find that this emphatic index downstroke flicked out against the thumb is widely used in other *toques* to give extra crispness and attack to the rhythm. You could, for example, introduce it on some of the accented beats in the *toques* you have already learned.

15.2 Flicking out the index against the thumb for extra emphasis.

A longer *rasgueo* roll is played in the third rhythm *compás* between *falsetas* 2 and 3 (in bar C in the music). Three 4-stroke *rasgueos* are played in succession without a break in the rhythm of the strokes of the fingers. The *rasgueo* starts on the count of 1 with a stroke by the little finger and the final index finger downstroke brings it to an end exactly on beat 3.

In the notation the figures 11/2 are written over the *rasgueo* to show that the first 11 strokes (**e a m i e a m i e a m**) take up the duration of two beats. This needs precise timing.

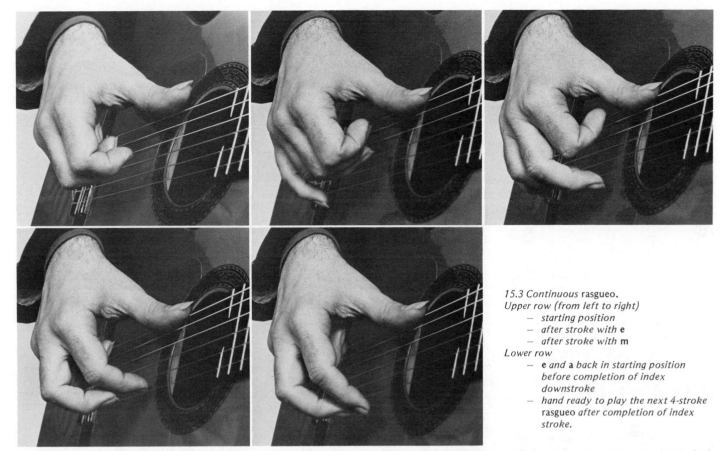

15.3 Continuous *rasgueo*.
Upper row (from left to right)
 — *starting position*
 — *after stroke with* **e**
 — *after stroke with* **m**
Lower row
 — **e** *and* **a** *back in starting position before completion of index downstroke*
 — *hand ready to play the next 4-stroke* rasgueo *after completion of index stroke.*

Photo sequence 15.3 shows how the fingers move when the 4-stroke *rasgueos* are repeated to produce an extended or continuous roll. Before the index finger completes its downstroke the little finger and ring finger have already moved back to their starting positions, ready to begin the next 4-stroke *rasgueo* without interruption to the rhythm. For a smooth continuous roll all the fingers are in motion, each one moving downwards across the strings and then back to its starting position and downwards again at a constant speed. The movements are coordinated in sequence so that the sound of the downstrokes continues in a regular and unbroken roll.

You will find it hard initially to play the three 4-stroke *rasgueos* in the solo rapidly and evenly enough for there to be no interruption or irregularity in the rhythm. To begin with you may find it easier to play the first two beats as 5-stroke *rasgueos*.

Fourth Bulerías

Cejilla at 2nd fret

95

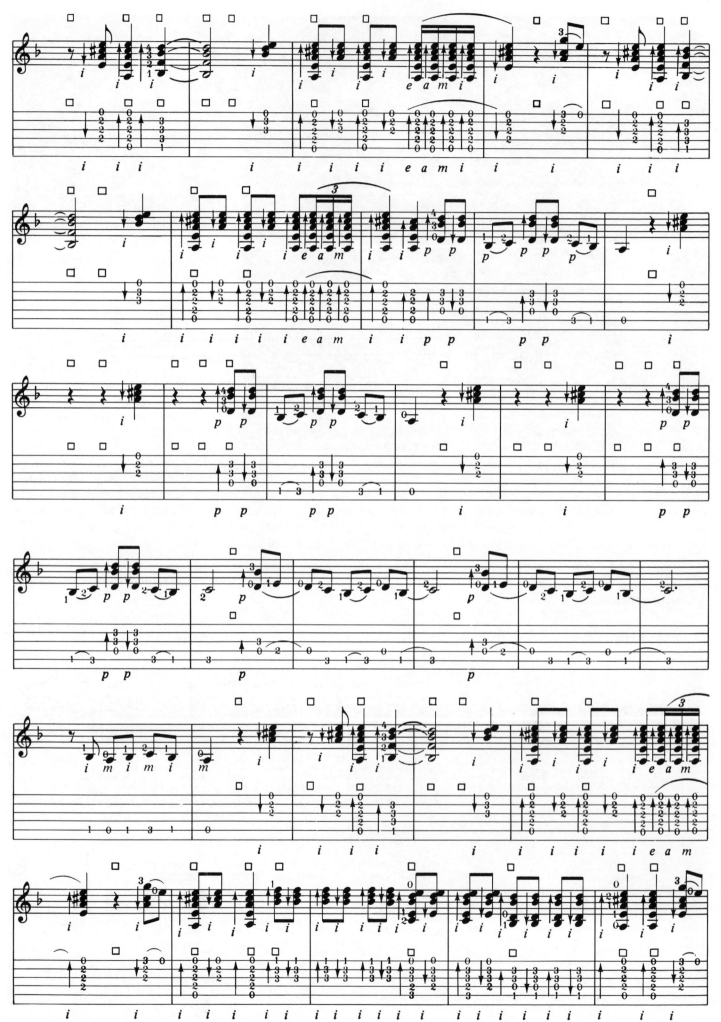

96

97

98

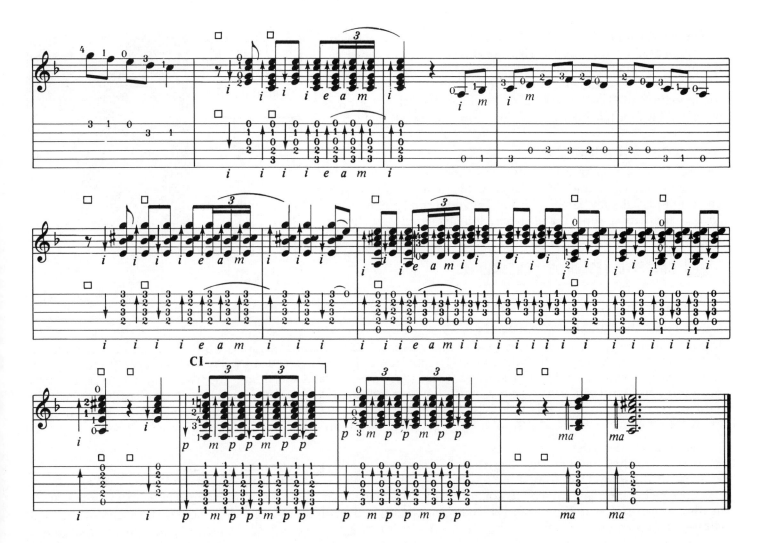

Observing the silences

Throughout the Bulerías it is absolutely essential that the duration of the silences, no less than of the sounds, should be very exactly timed, otherwise that crucial pulse of the *compás* will be lost. A particular illustration of this is the sequence D to E in the music. Here, a chord sequence of D minor, C and B♭ is played, the sound of each chord being abruptly quenched by *apagado* with the right hand. The chords must be played very strictly *a compás*.

Once you have mastered all the *falsetas* and rhythm passages in the Bulerías solos 1—4, you can try to fit them together to make a single solo piece. You will need to choose just one of the introductory *rasgueos* to start it off, and you can arrange the order of the *falsetas* in any way that seems most appropriate.

LESSON 16   Granadinas

Granadinas, or as the flamencos say *grana'inas*, are a form of Fandangos Grandes from the ancient city of Granada. In both their *cante* and *toque* they have a richly embellished and oriental quality which reflects early Moorish influences on the music from which they take root, for Granada was under the domination of the Moors from 711 A.D. to 1492.

Lyrical and intricately ornamented, the music of the *Toque por Granadinas* makes a beautiful guitar solo, full of sentiment and yearning nostalgia. If you have seen Granada, you will recognise how vividly Granadinas evoke the images and sounds of that magical city — the filligree-like decorations of its great Moorish fortress and palace the Alhambra, the snow-covered peaks of the surrounding Sierra Nevada and the tinkling music of the many streams bringing snow-water from the mountains. Here is music that is animated and inspired by the oriental *aire* of old Andalucía.

The COMPÁS

Much of the music for Granadinas is played *en toque libre* (in free time) without a regular *compás* and allowing the performer great freedom of personal expression and tempo. As in Fandangos Grandes, however, there are parts of the music in regular rhythm. These are written in 3/4 time. As in Fandangos, also, many of the melodic phrases in these rhythmic passages are 6 beats long (here represented by two bars of music).

The Phrygian mode used in Granadinas is unique in Flamenco in being based on the note B. The flamenco cadence of chords is therefore E minor (or E7), D major (or D7), C major (or C7) B major (or B with added E) or B7. The position of the left hand for the chord of B major with E on the open 1st string is shown in 16.1. The chord diagrams show this chord and E minor and B7.

The solo Granadinas

The music which follows is in typical Granadinas solo form. It includes a variety of traditional *falsetas*. These are mostly based on techniques already familiar to you, including *arpegio*, *picado*, *ligado*, alternating thumb and index, thumb *apoyando*, 3-note chords and *trémolo*.

CASSETTE: LESSON 16, GRANADINAS

B major (+ E)

E minor

B7 (alt. fingerings)

16.1 B major (+ E) for Granadinas.

glissando

Three new techniques are introduced in the solo.

1. The TRÉMOLO thumbstroke (i a m i $\stackrel{\uparrow}{p}$)

The introduction to the solo, as is typical of many Granadinas, starts with chords of B (with E) and C major played with a downward sweep of the right thumb. Each of these chords is preceded by a very rapid succession of *tirando* strokes, played with **i a m i** as in the *trémolo*, on the highest note of the chord. The hand is in the 'basic' position and the **i a m i** strokes (here written as grace notes to indicate that they precede the main emphasis on the chord) must be even and very rapid, leading into the chord without any irregularity or delay in the timing. You will need to practise them very slowly at first in order to get the timing right.

2. The long GLISSANDO

A left hand technique very characteristic of Granadinas is a long accelerating slide *(glissando)* up the 6th string from F♯ at the second fret to B at the seventh fret. The 2nd finger stops the string. After the string has been struck just once (with the right thumb) to sound the F♯, the pressure of the finger is maintained as it is slid up the string to the seventh fret. The slide from F♯ to B is notated as shown above. The glissando comes at the end of the final phrase of *falsetas* in Granadinas (which has similarities to a slow ending to Fandangos, though of course in a different key). Sometimes (but not in this solo) it is more appropriate for the 1st finger to be used.

3. ARRASTRE

The technique of *arrastre* (literally 'dragging'), is commonly used not only in Granadinas but in some other *toques* like the Tarantas. It is shown at the point marked A in the music. With the right hand in the 'basic' position, the hand is drawn upwards by slight bending of the forearm so that the fingernail of the flexed third finger is pulled back across the strings towards you, striking them *apoyando* in even succession from 1st to 6th. This sounds a rapid *arpegio* chord from treble to bass.

GRANADINAS

Cejilla at 2nd fret

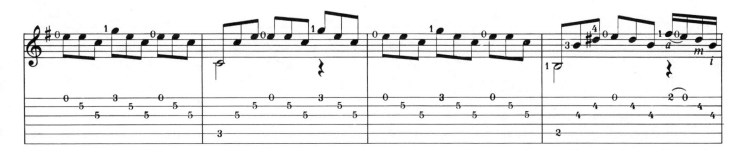

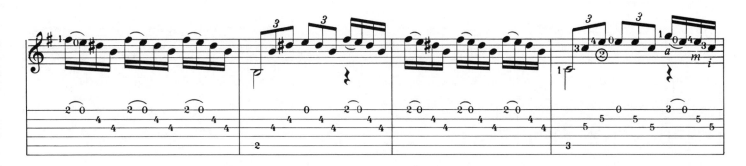

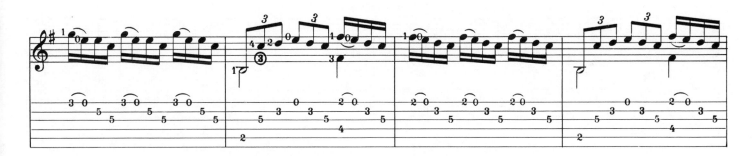

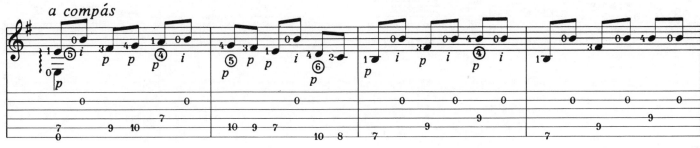

slowly

faster, *a compás*

103

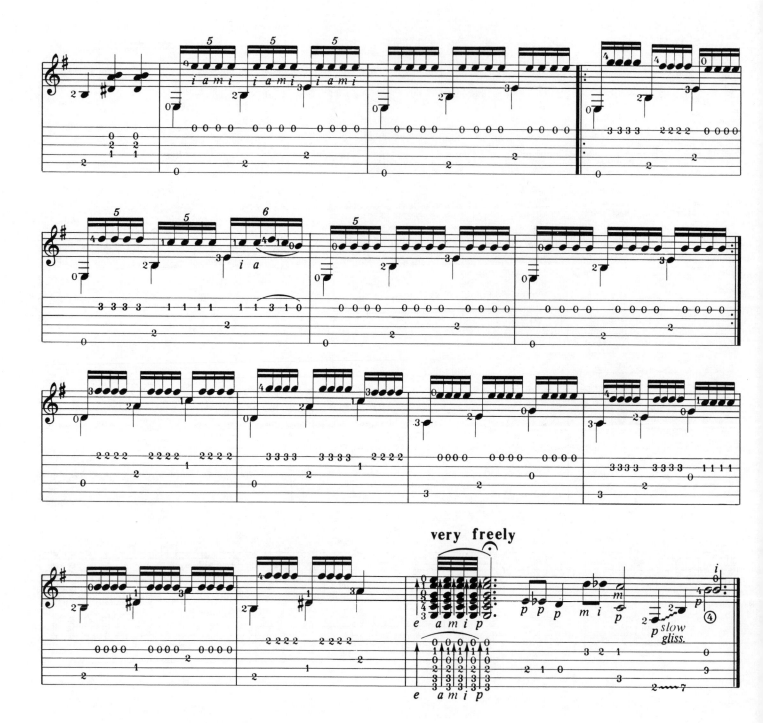

Further examples of the TRÉMOLO thumbstroke

This flamenco technique, illustrated in the introduction to the Granadinas, will be encountered again in Tientos, Malagueñas, Soleares and Alegrías *en Mi*. You might also like to introduce it at this stage as an alternative way of playing the introductory chords in the *Campanas* of the Alegrías in Lesson 6. The five A minor and five E7 chords at the beginning were initially played with sweeps of the thumb. You could now play them with the rapid i a m i *trémolo* on the top string preceding each chord, as follows:

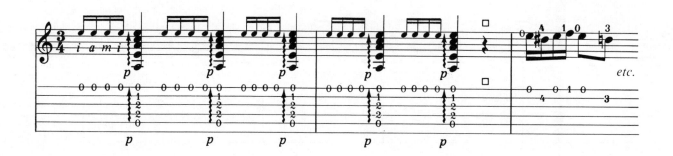

Elements of Flamenco 12   Improvisation

Parts of the Granadinas solo are *en toque libre* and you will have read in the music the direction that these are to be played 'very freely'. The freedom referred to is freedom from a strictly regular beat to the rhythm so that the player can interpret the music with the timing and phrasing he prefers. This is just one example of the several kinds of freedom the guitarist has opportunity for in his playing. It gives us an appropriate moment to look more widely at other kinds of freedom in the performance of the flamenco guitar.

The difference between improvisation and innovation

Flamenco music on the guitar is said to be 'improvised' because the guitarist is not limited by having to play to a predetermined routine or to a written score. He is free to play what he likes, but this does not mean, as is sometimes supposed, that he invents the music as he goes along. He makes it up by a process of choice rather than by instant innovation, by choosing *falsetas, rasgueos* and other linking passages from his pre-existing repertoire of well-practised items.

The experienced performer will know many different versions and variants of the *falsetas* and *rasgueos* he plays. He can piece these bits together in different ways to suit the *aire* of the *toque* and according to the mood and context of the moment. As a result, he may seldom repeat the performance of any *toque* in quite the same way. On some occasions he may rehearse carefully in advance exactly what he is going to do but on other occasions, particularly the more informal, he will play as the feeling takes him. In either case he is free to vary the selection and sequence of items from his repertoire, provided always that he sticks to the *compás* of the *toque* he is performing and, if he is playing for accompaniment, that he responds to the needs of the singer or dancer.

Individual players will obviously vary a lot in their creativeness and in the range and flexibility of their *toque*. Early on in his career, a guitarist will collect together the material for his repertoire by imitating and adapting music he has heard performed by other guitarists. Later, if he has some gifts as a composer, he will add variations which he has invented himself. Eventually, after he has had long experience, the working repertoire from which he draws the music he performs may become largely (and for some pieces, entirely) made up of his own original inventions.

By 'innovation' or 'invention' we mean here the art of creating new music for the guitar. It is not something which usually takes place while the guitarist is actually performing before an audience. Sometimes, it is true, he may be exceptionally inspired, perhaps by a particular occasion such as a *juerga* (flamenco celebration) or an especially moving performance by a singer, to bring off some new variation in his playing. But these moments of sudden intuition are likely to be rare in public. Innovation is a private thing, which can occur when the guitarist explores new ideas and possibilities while he is alone with his instrument.

Learning to improvise

The keen student of Flamenco must have a good grasp of basic techniques for the guitar and a repertoire of well-rehearsed material before he can go very far towards improvising his own solos. He does not have to have a very extensive repertoire of *falsetas* and *rasgueos* to choose from, but he must have a real feeling for the *aire* of those that he does know if he is to arrange them in a musical and flamenco way. To play just a random miscellany of *falsetas* and *rasgueos* in a *toque* is not enough to make a worthwhile solo. They should lead on from one another to make an emotionally meaningful sequence, so that there is some overall sense of form and development in the performance.

It is, of course, difficult to formulate rules about how to do this. One can state definitely that too much *trémolo* will sap any *toque* of its flamenconess, making it insipid and too far removed from the essential inspiration of the *Cante* and *Baile*. It is, by contrast, far harder to state how much rhythmic *rasgueo* one should include in solos. Some players intersperse their *falsetas* with quite a lot of *rasgueo* in order to generate a driving pulsation and drama in the music and to stay close to the form and spirit of flamenco singing and dancing, but other soloists include little or hardly any. The choice is up to you.

There is probably little or nothing to be said briefly about how one goes about creating new *falsetas* and *rasgueos* which are to have any lasting interest or appeal, for it is a process which is only possible on the basis of a long familiarity and deep understanding of Flamenco. If your ultimate ambitions lie in this direction, however, you can make a start by trying to learn as much material as you can from available sources so that you can acquire a wide knowledge of the musical components and techniques from which Flamenco has been created. The technical aspects are more easily learned than the musical, but the latter are much the most important. Your left hand must know the fingerboard well (so that you can, for example, play chords in many inversions up and down the neck) and your right hand must know the many ways the strings can be struck in different rhythmic patterns. Above all, though, you should look to the inspiration of the *Cante* in your search for the ingredients from which one day, if you pursue your interest in Flamenco far enough, you can hope to make new inventions.

LESSON 17   Tientos

Tangos are a basic form of flamenco rhythm in 4/4 (or 2/4) time, probably originating from Cádiz and Sevilla but heard now throughout Andalucía. Tientos are the most solemn and profound *cante* and *toque* of the group and they are distinguished from the faster styles of Tangos by their characteristic *compás* and by their serious themes. The word *tiento* literally means a 'touch'.

The flamenco Tangos have nothing in common with the Latin-American tango apart from the name. The most lightweight and least intense of the flamenco family of Tangos are the Tanguillos, which are tuneful folk-songs and dances in 6/8 time, particularly associated with Cádiz. The many kinds of Tangos may be known by a rather confusing variety of names such as *tangos flamencos, tangos gitanos* and *tangos* (or *tientos*) *canasteros.* Some styles have much in common with the Zambras. Some of the *Zambras del Sacromonte,* for instance, played by the *gitanos* of Granada are in the rhythm of slow Tangos.

The music of Tientos is played on the guitar in the *por medio* position (the Phrygian mode based on A). In addition to the familiar flamenco progression of chords (D minor or F, C(7), B♭, A), there are some *falsetas* where the chords follow *coplas* of the *cante.* Often a singer will end his performance of Tientos with a faster Tangos.

The COMPÁS

The strict *compás* of Tientos is distinguished by its characteristic pattern of emphasis and syncopation. This imparts a strongly 'lamenting' quality, full of sadness and pathos, yet dignified by strength and grandeur. The feeling can be deeply moving and *jondo.*

The first sequence of Tientos played on the cassette-recording demonstrates the basic *compás* in its simplest form. The method of counting the *compás* is shown with the musical notation, below. The rhythm is played with down and upstrokes of the index on the chords of A major, B♭ (with E on the open 1st string) D minor and C major. You should start by listening to the recording carefully until you have the sound of the rhythm firmly fixed in your mind. You will then be able to study the notation so that you can play it with the correct timing, accentuation and *aire.*

> 🔲 CASSETTE : **LESSON 17, TIENTOS, THE BASIC COMPÁS**

Tientos: the basic COMPÁS

Cejilla at 3rd fret

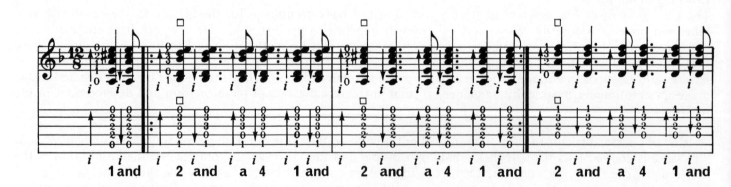

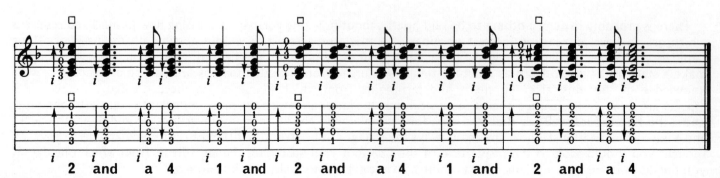

The notation of the COMPÁS of Tientos

The traditional flamenco way of learning Tientos (as with other kinds of *compás*) is by imitation and by counting the rhythm aloud, rather than from written notation or by a theoretical analysis of its structure. Since, however, you will be studying it from notation as well as by listening to the cassette-recording, a detailed explanation of the way the rhythm has been notated is provided here.

It will help you to understand the basic *compás* of Tientos and its representation on paper if you relate the rhythm to a repeated pattern of 4 beats, counted as a steady 1 − 2 − 3 − 4 − 1 − 2 − 3 − 4 etc. In notation, this pattern of 4 beats could be written in a time-signature of 4/4 as follows:

The accents of the *compás* fall unvaryingly on the counts of 2 and 4. For this reason, and also because of the timing of changes of chord, the bar-lines are placed between beats 1 and 2.

If each of these 4 counted beats is subdivided into two, we have:

This is the rhythm of Tangos. The *compás* of Tientos introduces two modifications into this simple rhythm. They are all-important if your playing of Tientos is to capture the expressive *aire* of the modern *toque*.

The first modification is that in Tientos the beats are often divided into three rather than two. In other words, parts of the rhythm are in 'compound' time and parts are in 'simple' time. A way to represent this clearly is to write the basic pattern of 4 beats in 12/8 time rather than 4/4. Each crotchet beat in 4/4 time is represented in 12/8 as a dotted crotchet

The duration of the beats and bars is not altered by this change of time-signature, so we can write:

In Tientos there is a very characteristic timing of the two chords (or single notes) played within the duration of the beat counted as 1. In 12/8 time the time-values of these two chords can be represented accurately by a crotchet followed by a quaver:

The second modification is a characteristic syncopation in the first half of each bar. Instead of   as the first two beats of the bar in 12/8 time we have   or, as it will be written here for the sake of clarity,

You can now understand why the count of 3 has been left out of the traditional method of counting shown earlier with the music: the second chord of the bar (played with an index upstroke) anticipates by one third of a beat the count of 3 in a steady count of 1−2−3−4. 12/8 time again allows this to be clearly shown.

The basic *compás* of Tientos can now be written in 12/8 time as:

The timing of the 'and' after the count of 1, and of the 'and a' after 2 must be carefully observed.

A common mistake is to cut short the duration of the beat on the count of 4 so that the rhythm becomes:

This destroys the *compás* of Tientos.

The solo

The longer Tientos solo which now follows is made up of traditional *falsetas* and *rasgueo*. You will see that 5-stroke *rasgueos* have been introduced into the rhythm sequences. The *rasgueos* start on the quaver indicated previously by the count of 'a' in the '2 and a' which corresponds to the syncopation just described. The accent of each *rasgueo* falls on the final index upstroke, which coincides exactly with the count of 4.

In one of the *falsetas* the melody is played in a simple 4/4 rhythm (the time-signature is shown in the music) rather than 12/8. In the bars of 4/4 one crotchet has the same duration as one dotted crotchet in the bars of 12/8.

 CASSETTE: THE SOLO TIENTOS

Cejilla at 3rd fret

TIENTOS

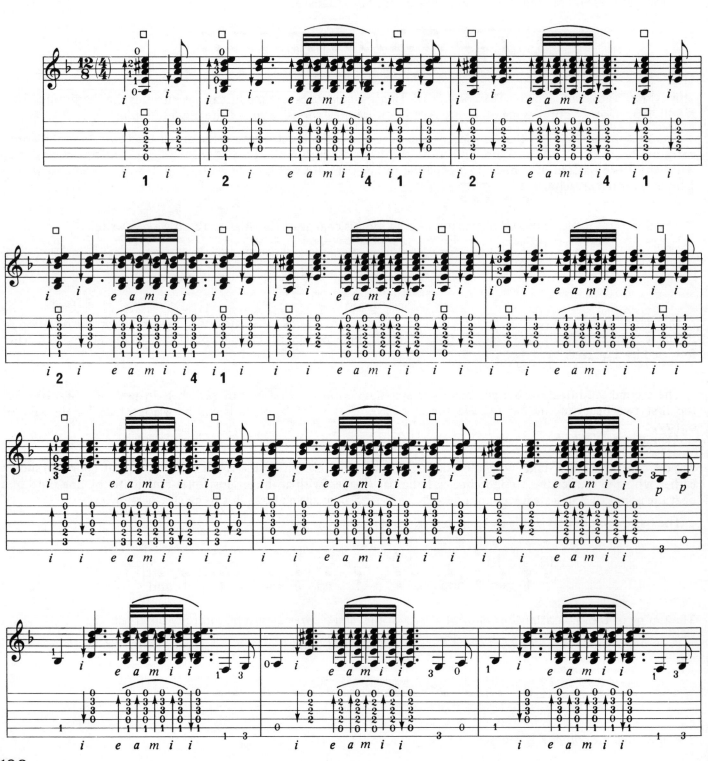

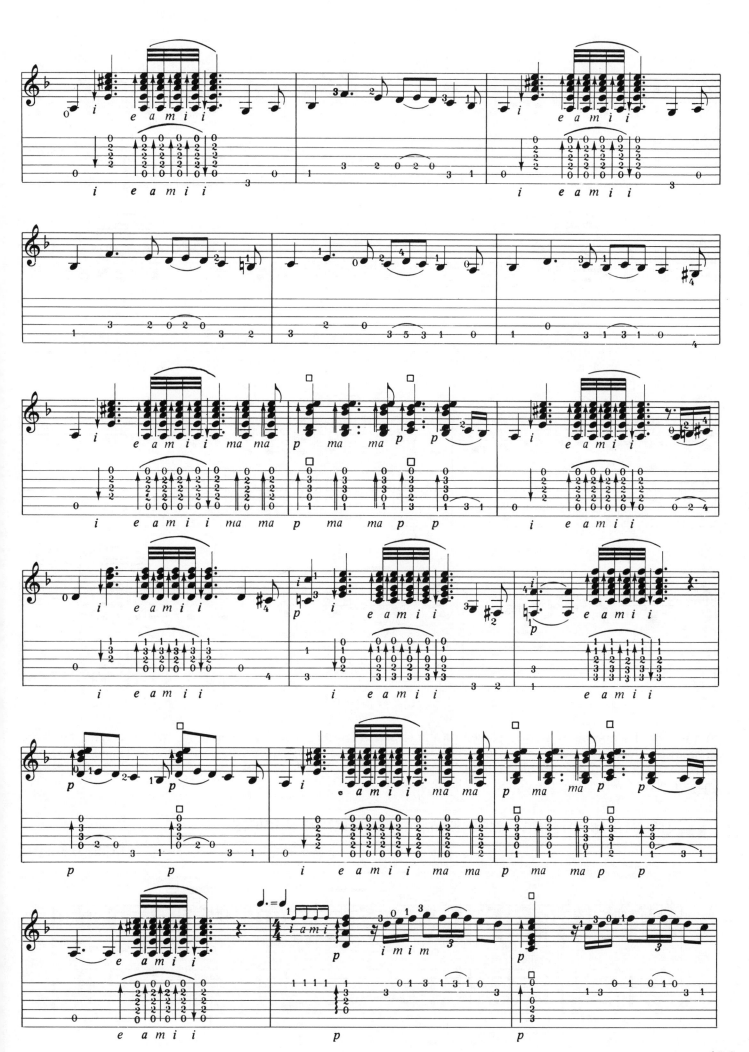

109

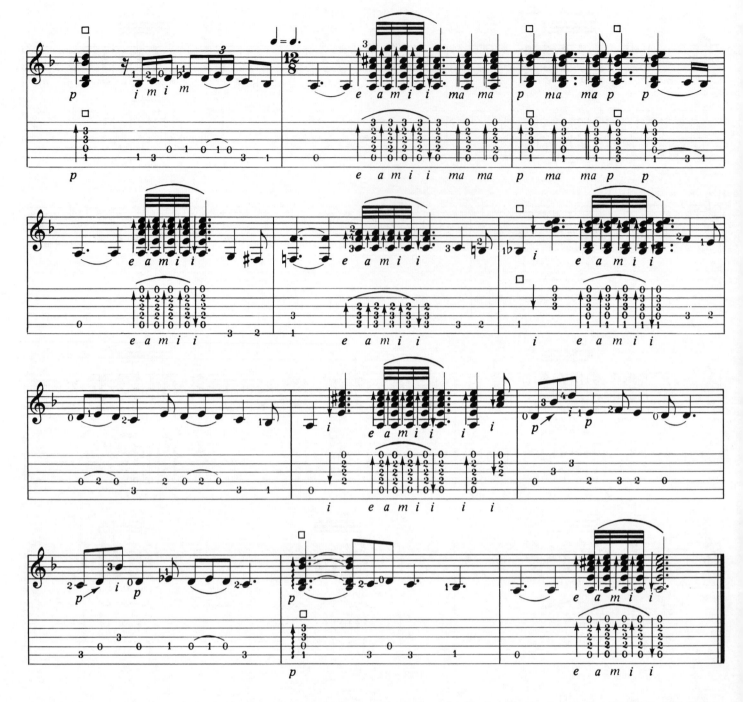

A third brief sequence of Tientos played on the cassette-recording shows an alternative way of playing the basic *compás* of Tientos, as heard in the solo. You will see from the notation that strokes with middle and third finger together are used to give added emphasis in the downstrokes. The downstroke on the count of 2 in the first bar may be played with either the thumb or with **m** and **a** together.

📼 **CASSETTE: AN ALTERNATIVE WAY OF PLAYING THE BASIC COMPÁS OF TIENTOS**

The section between the repeat signs may be repeated as many times as appropriate: the pattern of right hand strokes can be played with the left hand chord changes illustrated in the first version of the basic compás. *The final chord will fall on the beat of 4 marked with an asterisk,* ✱.

Cejilla at 3rd fret

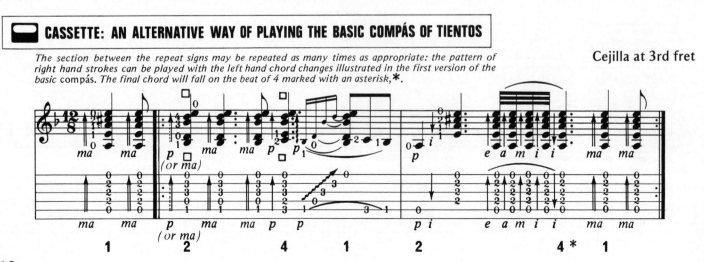

LESSON 18 Zapateado

Zapateado, literally meaning 'tapped with the shoe', is a general term for the footwork with *punta y tacón* ('point and heel') in the flamenco *Baile*. It is also the name of a specific dance, a virtuoso solo for a man which provides a display of his speed and control in the *taconeo*. The music for this dance is played to the rhythm of the Tanguillo in 6/8 time (alternatively notated as triplets in 2/4 time) and the *toque* is usually in the chord positions of the key of C major. The basic chords, therefore, are C major, F major and G7. Other major keys (e.g. E major) are sometimes used. Although not a profound *toque*, the Zapateado can be a delightfully tuneful and rhythmic guitar solo which can show off guitar techniques such as *picado* particularly well.

The COMPÁS is strictly regular, with a characteristic pulse in the rhythm, notated here as 2/4 time for the linking passages of *rasgueo* and 6/8 for the *falsetas*. There are also changes in tempo which reflect the different variations of the dance. Accelerations to a climax are followed by passages at a slower speed and then a building up again of the tempo. In some versions there may be passages in the more sombre minor key (the tonic minor) and modulations to other keys.

The solo is made up of *rasgueos* and *falsetas* which follow a traditional pattern on a basis of C major, F major and G7 chords. All the techniques used have been described previously. It is entitled *Zapateado para bailar* ('for dancing') because it typifies the traditional accompaniment to the dance.

CASSETTE: LESSON 18, ZAPATEADO

ZAPATEADO para bailar

Cejilla at 2nd Fret

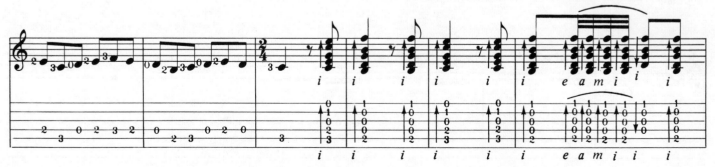

114

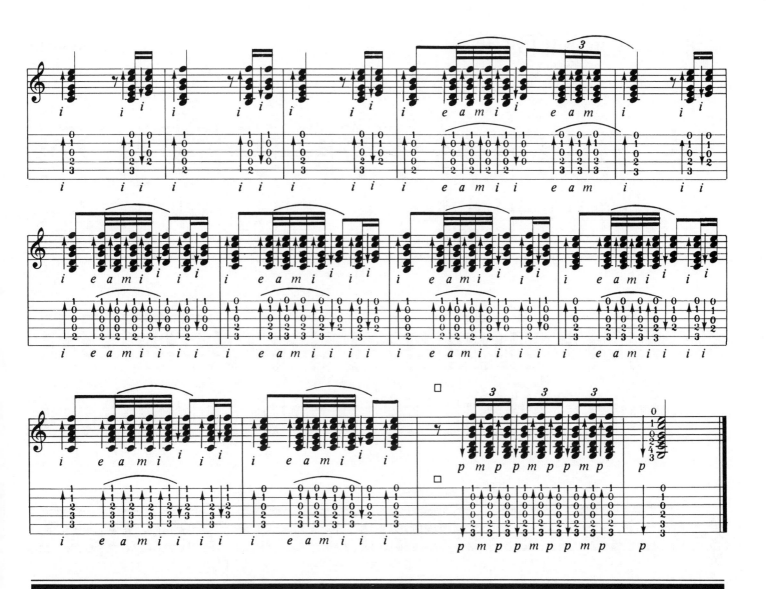

LESSON 19   Soleá por medio

The Soleá por medio (like the closely related Soleá por Bulerías) is a *toque* derived from Soleares, which has similarities to earlier styles of Bulerías. Played in the *por medio* position and intermediate in tempo between Soleares and the modern Bulerías, the *toque* has an urgent and intense *aire* all its own.

The solo here is played in a typical *gitano* style, with a variety of *rasgueo* interludes between the *falsetas* maintaining the strongly driving rhythm.

    It provides good examples of the triplet *alzapúa* (indicated in the music) and also makes frequent use of a very flamenco *arpegio* technique in the *falsetas* and ending phrases. A bass melody is played with the thumb *apoyando*. The first beat of each melodic phrase of three beats is played as a double *arpegio* and the second and third are played with 'forward' *arpegios* (**i m a**). The rhythm of the *arpegios* is important. When the 'back' arpegio (**p a m i**) was introduced in Lesson 3 it was stressed that the four notes should be in absolutely even rhythm without any delay after the initial thumbstroke. Here, by contrast, there is such a delay on the emphatic thumbstroke as you will hear clearly in the recording. The special rhythmic character of the *arpegios* is not easily conveyed in notation.

In this solo (and in later ones where the same technique is used) the time-values of the notes in each *arpegio* are written as shown on the right, indicating that the three strokes with **i m a** start half a beat after the thumbstroke and together occupy the duration of half a beat. In fact, they may be delayed even later sometimes, so that together they take up less than half a beat, with the thumbstroke correspondingly prolonged in duration before the strokes with **i m a**. Careful listening to the recording will give you the correct timing.

🔲 **CASSETTE: LESSON 19, SOLEÁ POR MEDIO**

115

SOLEÁ POR MEDIO

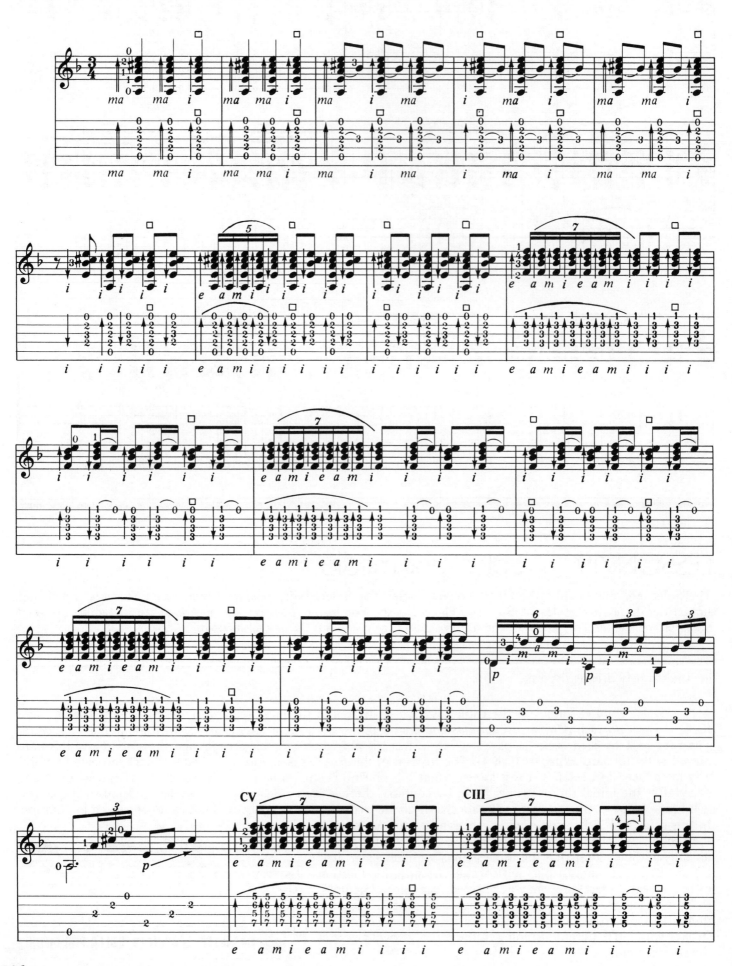

116

LESSON 20   Malagueñas

In Málaga the Fandango has evolved into many styles of Malagueñas, whose *coplas* range in feeling from deepest tragedy to carefree good humour. The Malagueña, therefore, has been called a *Cante Intermedio*, a *cante* that is intermediate between the *Jondo* and the *Chico*. The really gifted singer can perform Malagueñas in a movingly *jondo* way, with an *aire* that approaches the intensity of Soleares, but there are also much lighter styles which celebrate the joys of life and the beauties of the countryside.

The flamenco *cantes* heard today date back to the end of the last century. Their development from the simple country melodies of Málaga such as the rhythmic songs and dances called Verdiales can be attributed to the innovations of several outstanding *malagueñeros*. Three creators of Malagueñas became particularly famous, Antonio Ortega (who called himself 'Juan El Breva'), Enrique Jiménez ('El Mellizo') and Don Antonio Chacón. Each in his turn brought increasing complexity and sophistication to his *cante*, gaining widespread renown and a host of imitators. Their styles of Malagueñas are known today by their names.

The COMPÁS
As Malagueñas developed, the rhythm became freer, the melodies more elaborately ornamented. In the forms of Malagueñas played today the rhythm is partly *en toque libre* and partly in a regular 3/4 time, with many echoes of

120

the Fandango. The music is in the Phrygian mode based on E.

The solo

The solo Malagueñas played here illustrates a very freely improvised style of *toque*, with an introduction and finale in free time together with *falsetas* in regular rhythm. The first *falseta* has a melody in chords and *ligado* and the second is an extended passage of rapid alternating thumb and index strokes. Note carefully, in the first *falseta*, the way the melody is syncopated. In the second, you will see that in the earlier bars thumb and index are played simultaneously on the third beat of the bar, whereas they alternate throughout the later parts of the melody.

The introduction *en toque libre* (with a first part here in an alternating 3/4:6/8 rhythm) begins on a chord of E7. The music will look daunting at first, but it has been notated to show in detail three long rolls played with repeated 4-stroke *rasgueos*, interspersed with fast index down- and upstrokes. The first two long rolls are played with the **e a m i** sequence of strokes repeated to a total of five times, and the third, during which the left hand changes the chord to F major, contains ten 4-stroke *rasgueos* in continuous sequence. It is important in these continued *rasgueos* that the fingers should strike the strings in even rhythm so that there is no interruption between one 4-stroke sequence and the next.

CASSETTE: LESSON 20, MALAGUEÑAS

MALAGUEÑAS

Cejilla at 3rd fret

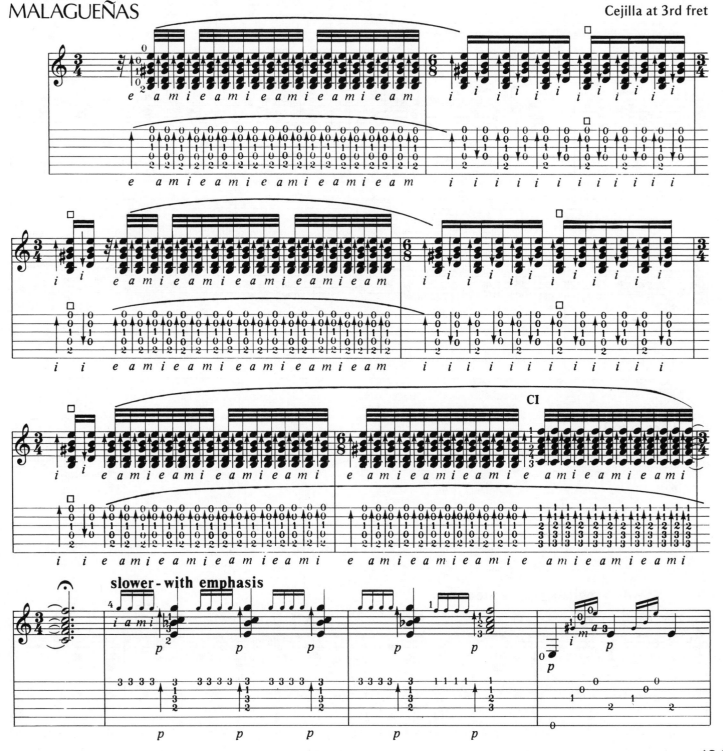

123

LESSON 21 Tarantos

People of the province of Almería have been popularly known as *tarantos*. As a flamenco *cante* and *toque* the Taranto is a strongly rhythmic style closely related to Tarantas, a form of Fandango Grande originating from Almería and neighbouring provinces of the Spanish Levante such as Jaen and Murcia. The towns of Almería, Linares and Cartagena are major centres. Tarantas are a *toque libre* but Tarantos have a strictly regular and emphatic *compás* in 2/4 or 4/4 time.

Tarantas probably have early roots in the popular folk-music of these south-eastern provinces. The themes of the *coplas* are often narrative and very varied but there is in many of them (and still more in the closely related *cantes* of Mineras and Cartageneras) a special association with mining. The songs give tragic expression to the sorrows and deprivations of the miner's life. Some say that *Andaluz* labourers coming to work in the mines of La Unión brought these songs with them, but others believe that the *coplas* were originally local ones which became adapted to the flamenco style of *Cante*.

F♯ for Tarantos

21.1 F sharp chord for Tarantos.

Tarantos and Tarantas have a very oriental sound because of their harmonies and ornamentation. The music is in the Phrygian mode based on F sharp, with a highly characteristic dissonance produced by the basic chord pattern which has F♯ and C♯ on the three bass strings against three open treble strings to make the chord F♯ C♯ F♯ G B E. This chord and a version of G major on the lower four strings used in Tarantos are shown on the right.

The music is notated in the key signature of two sharps, i.e. D major or B minor. The flamenco cadence contains the chords B minor or D major, A major, G major, F♯ with G, B and E or F♯ major.

The solo

The solo begins with the typical chords and bass-string *ligados* of Tarantos or Tarantas. Traditional *falsetas* follow, played with thumb *apoyando* and *arpegio* and the final *falseta* is a *copla* in which the melody is played *apoyando* with an accompaniment of chords played with downstrokes. The rhythm throughout is marked and regular.

G major for Tarantos

21.2 G major for Tarantos.

124

TARANTOS

Cejilla at 3rd fret

CASSETTE: LESSON 21, TARANTOS

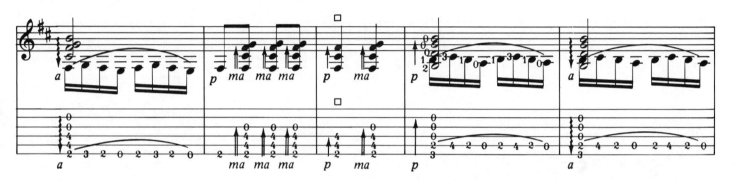

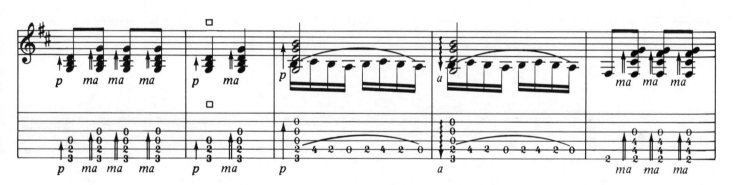

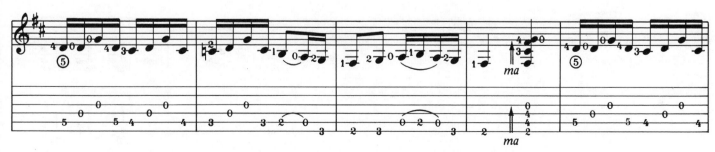

126

128

LESSON 22   Soleá

The solo Soleá comprising the music for this lesson is the first of four solo pieces which will advance your knowledge of essential *toques* you have already met earlier in the book.

In the solo there is an extended *falseta* with *arpegios* and chords in higher positions as well as other, traditional *falsetas*. The piece does not make very difficult technical demands but depends for its effect on the two essential elements of *compás* and *aire*. You should try to bring out the strong pulsation of the rhythm and the emotional meaning which motivates the music and which develops progressively through the linked sequences of *rasgueo* and *falsetas*. When you can do this, the solo will be a powerful expression of your basic feeling for Flamenco.

▭ **CASSETTE: LESSON 22, SOLEÁ**

SOLEÁ

Cejilla at 2nd Fret

130

Flamenco VIBRATO

In the flamenco technique of *vibrato* a left hand finger stopping a string pulls the string (after it has been sounded by the right hand) across the fingerboard towards the palm, in a direction parallel to the frets. The movement of the finger is a very rapid alternation of flexion and relaxation which is repeated several times to produce an up-and-down vibration of pitch in the note sounded, giving it a plaintive 'lamenting' quality. When the stopping finger pulls the string, the pitch of the note is sharpened; when it relaxes, the note returns to its natural pitch. The technique is particularly used for single melody notes on strings 5, 4 and 3 in such expressive *toques* as Soleares (e.g. on the accented bass notes of *arpegio falsetas*) or Malagueñas.

LESSON 23   Alegrías en Mi

Alegrías en Mi (i.e. in the key of E major) are also known as Rosas or Alegrías por Rosas. The *compás* is the same as in the Alegrías en La (in A major) of Lesson 6, but the different key imparts a darker, richer sound to the music. It is commonly played at a rather slower speed. The rhythm, and especially the examples of *contratiempo*, will need careful attention.

The passage in E minor introduced by the *Campanas* was being played in the *Corral de la Morería* (a well-known flamenco showplace and restaurant in Madrid) about 1963. It quickly became popular with other guitarists.

When the music returns to the major key, you will recognise the melody of the traditional *escobilla*. It is similar to the *escobilla* in Lesson 6, but is now transposed to the key of E and is embellished with double *arpegios*.

 CASSETTE: LESSON 23, ALEGRÍAS EN MI

ALEGRÍAS en Mi

Cejilla at 2nd Fret

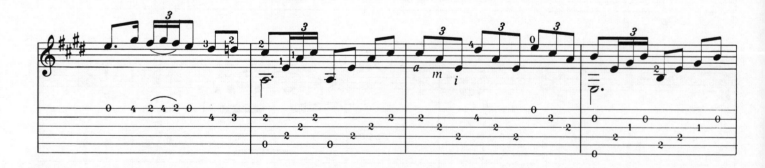

134

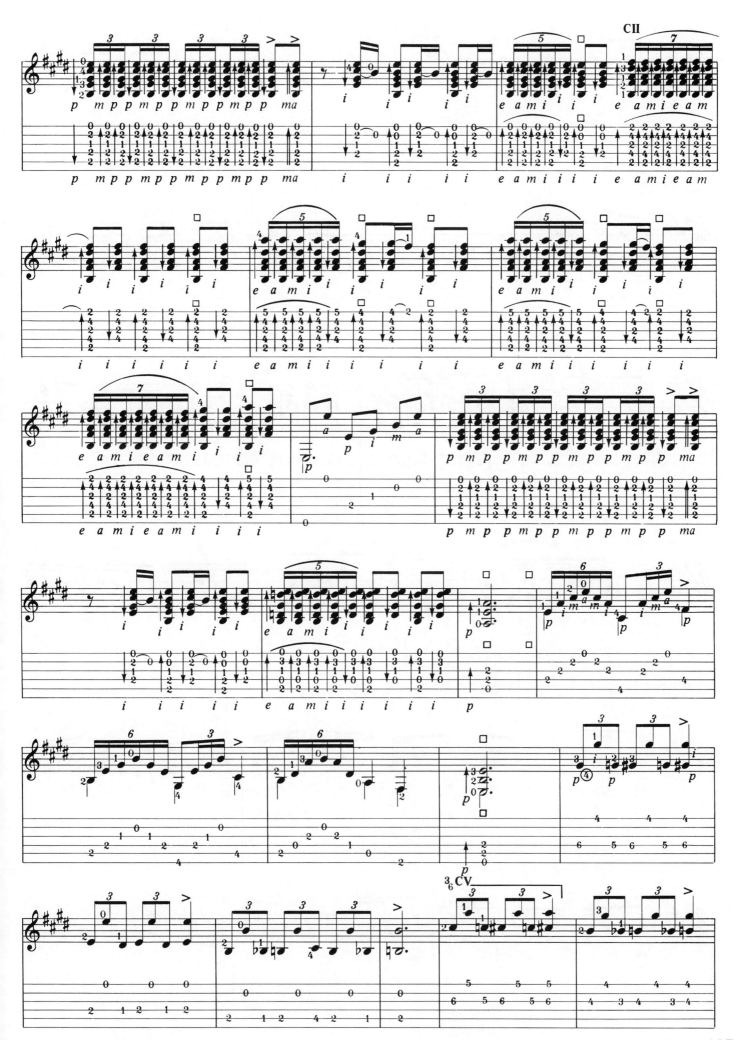

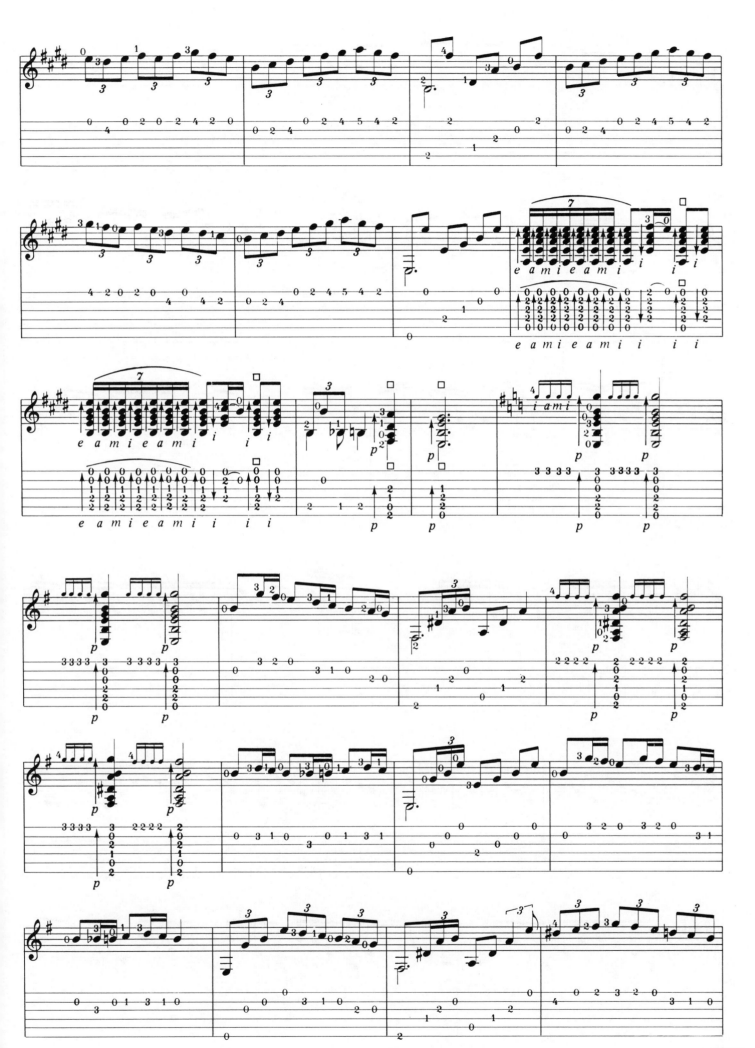

138

LESSON 24   Seguiriyas

The beautiful traditional *falsetas* of this solo powerfully communicate the tragic inspiration of Seguiriyas.

The introductory *rasgueo* and three later interludes of *rasgueo* demonstrate a characteristic pattern in Seguiriyas, with double 4-stroke *rasgueos* leading onto beats 4 and 5 of the *compás* described in Lesson 5. The first time the *rasgueos* are played all 5 upper strings are sounded. The next three times, only the lower strings are struck. The thumb resting on the 6th string prevents it from sounding a note, but the fingers hit across this string in the *rasgueo*, each making a distinct sound from the deadened string, rather like the beat of a snare-drum. This adds a characteristic sound to the staccato roll of the *rasgueo*.

 CASSETTE: LESSON 24, SEGUIRIYAS

SEGUIRIYAS

Cejilla at 3rd fret

140

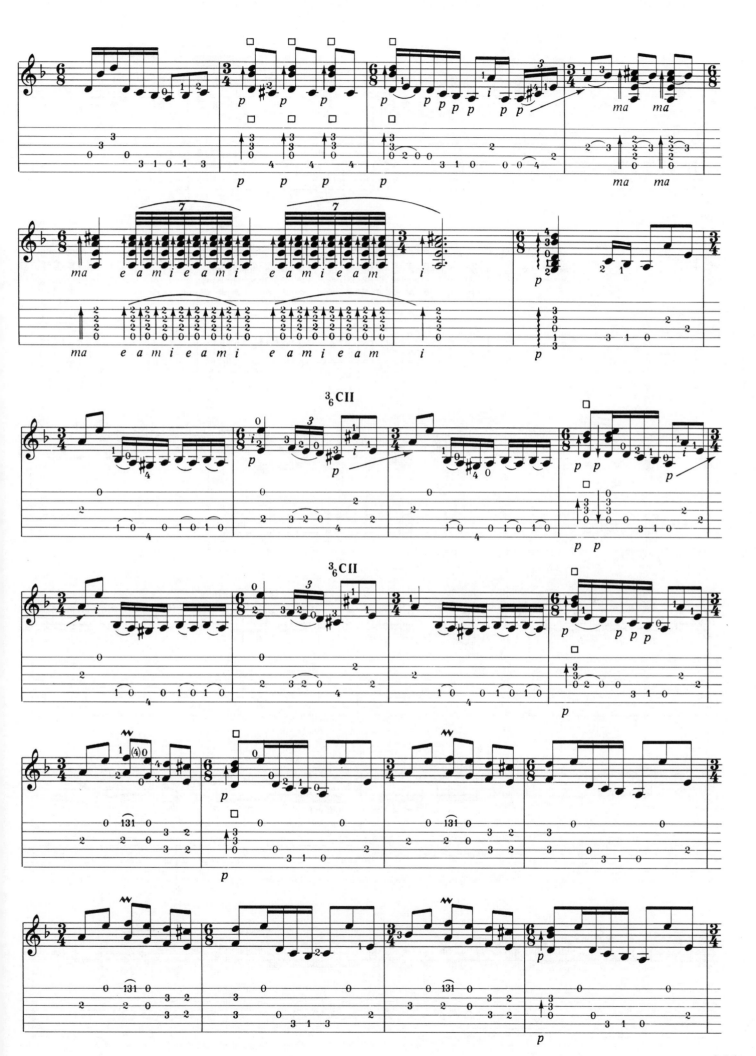

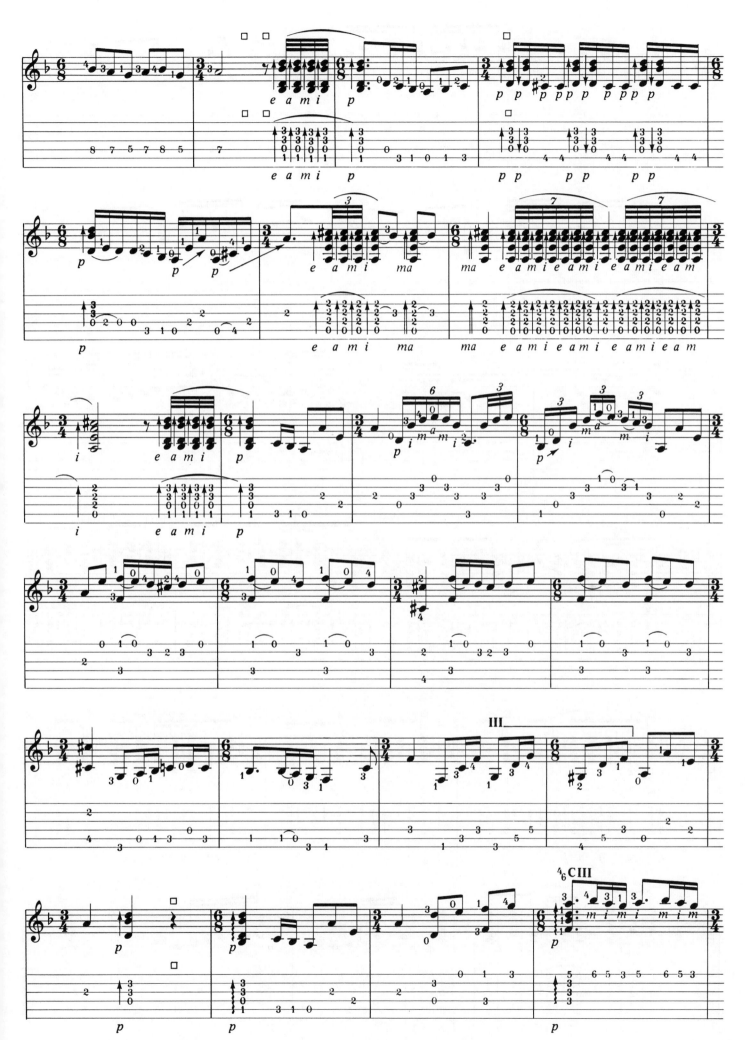

143

144

24.1 *Rafael Romero sings* por Seguiriyas.

The relationship between Seguiriyas and Soleares

There is an important relationship between the *compás* of Seguiriyas and that of Soleares. Possibly it accounts for the historical derivation of the Seguiriyas.

If you examine the *compás* of Seguiriyas carefully, you will find that the pattern of accentuation imposed on the 12 half-beats in the *compás* is the same as the pattern in the basic 12-beat *compás* of Soleares. The difference is that there has in effect been a shifting along of the accents so that beat 1 of Seguiriyas corresponds to beat 8 of Soleares. Starting from the 'and' after the count 3 in Seguiriyas and repeating the whole *compás* again we see that the *compás* of Soleares emerges as follows:

145

LESSON 25   Bulerías

The following solo for Bulerías begins in the Phrygian mode in *por medio*, modulates (i.e. changes key) to A minor and finishes in A major. Included among the *falsetas* and *rasgueo* sequences in these three keys are some new patterns of syncopation. All of them still fit within the basic framework of the repeating 12-beat *compás*. They provide further illustration of the many rhythmic variations which may be performed in this exciting *toque*. This time, the solo starts with a *falseta*, on the count of 1 in the *compás*.

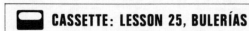 **CASSETTE: LESSON 25, BULERÍAS**

BULERÍAS

Cejilla at 2nd Fret

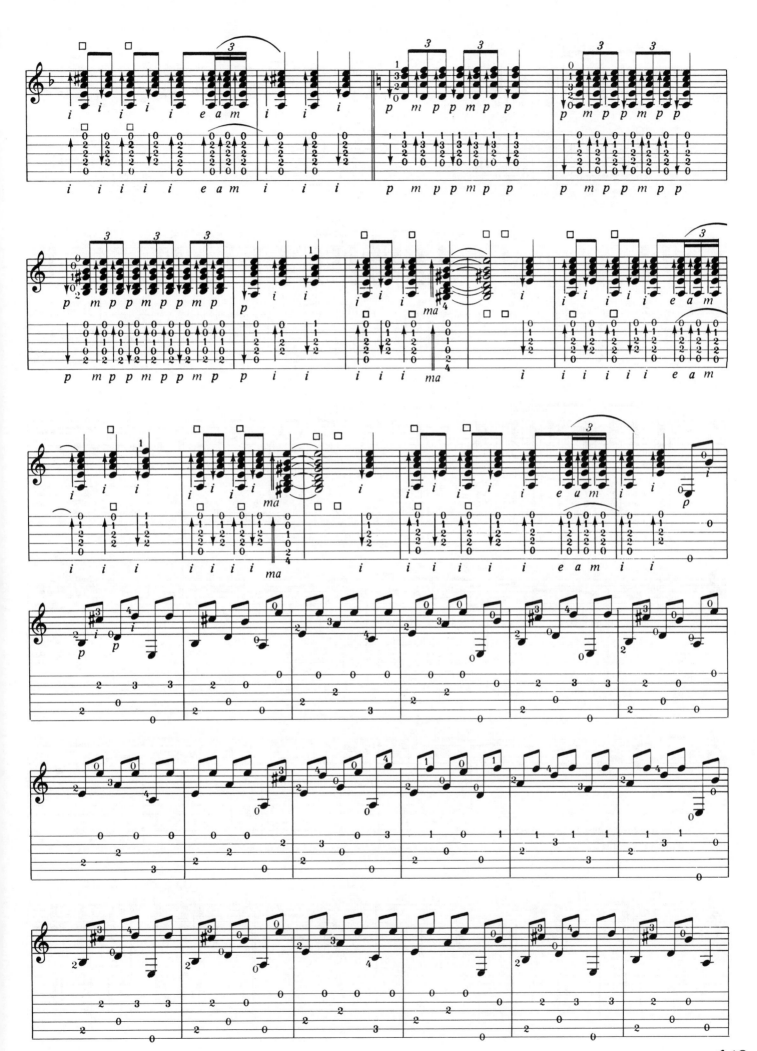

149

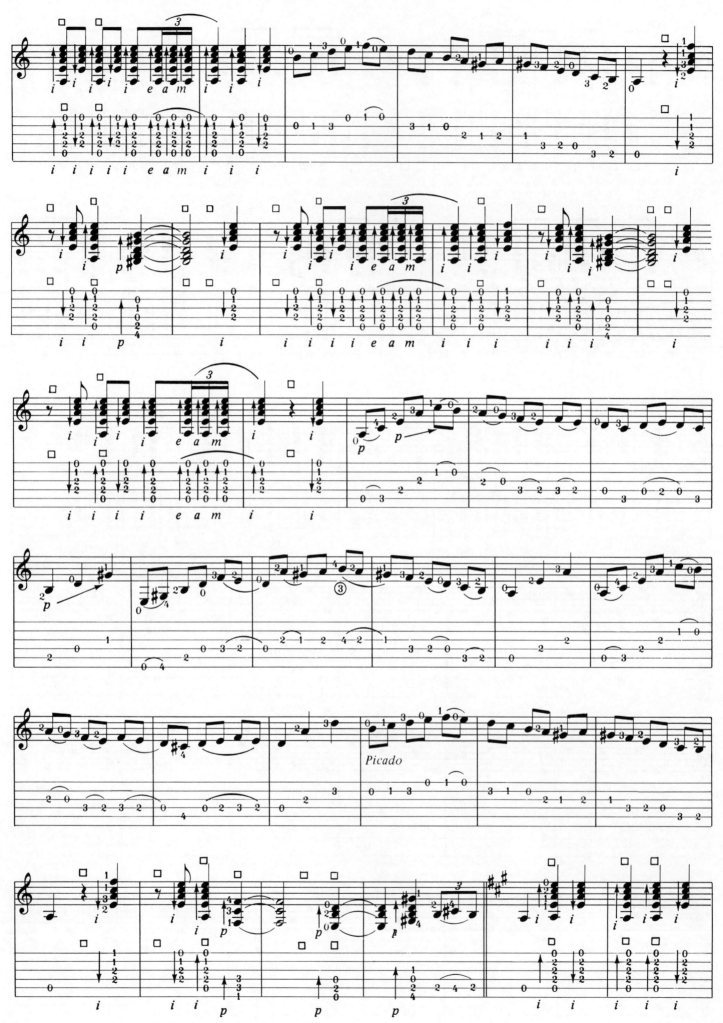

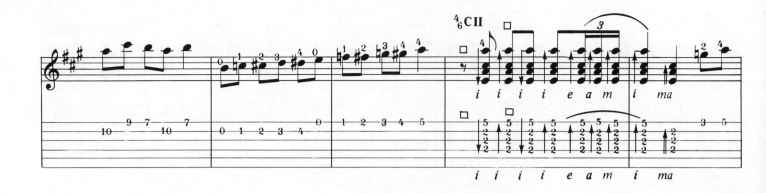

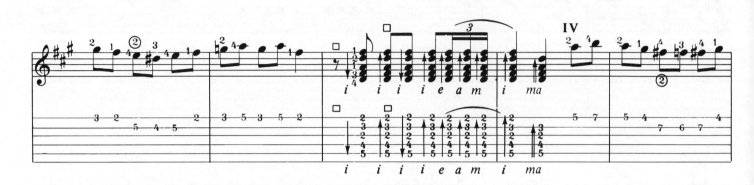

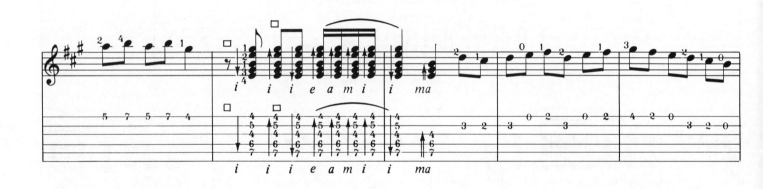

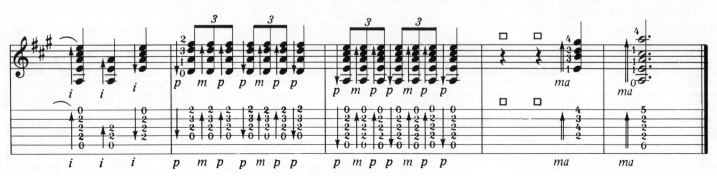

152

LESSON 26   Daily Exercises

Several exercises in the book have already been recommended as good for practising every day, however advanced you are. Some more are included here to help develop good basic techniques and also as a 'warm-up' for the hands when you first pick up your guitar.

Since your time for practice is likely to be limited, it is worth outlining first some general principles about how to make the most effective and rewarding use of whatever time you have. However high you have set your sights, whether you just want a modest degree of skill or are aiming for an advanced or even professional standard, your progress will be faster and further in the time available if your practice is purposeful and organised, with some definite aims in mind each time you play.

Principles of effective practice

1. Starting
Your hands need time to warm up, so it is important not to try to play at full speed and strength straight away. Build up slowly. Too sudden an exertion can strain muscles and tendons.

2. Directed energy: learning to relax
When you first try to achieve the muscular strength and coordination needed for Flamenco, it is natural to be inclined to apply your efforts in a general and rather undirected way. As a result, tension is likely to build up, perhaps without your being aware of it, in muscles in neighbouring and more distant parts of the body which should not be involved in the movement required. This misdirection of effort can be a bar to progress.

Effective practice actually involves learning which muscles to relax, no less importantly than which muscles to contract.

One learns to apply energy in an increasingly selective way, bringing the focus of effort into the hands and the exactly appropriate and most economical movement of the fingers. Less and less energy is wasted in irrelevant movements and muscles which should be relaxed if the focussed energy is to have most effect.

After hard practice, the muscles involved in the techniques you have been working on may ache from the exertion, particularly in the left hand fingers and the forearm muscles. Such discomfort is good evidence that you have been extending their power, but discomfort elsewhere in the body or a general feeling of tiredness and strain should warn you that energy is being misdirected. A good posture of the back and shoulders is especially important.

If you direct your energies accurately to where they are needed, practice becomes a fascinating exercise in coordinating thought and action. It should never be a dreary chore of laborious and mindless repetition. Time spent in purposeful practice will be generously repaid by progress, in very fair proportion to the amount of time you can devote to it.

3. Getting the basic techniques right
You may well feel by now that the importance of strictly keeping the *compás* has already been stressed enough in this book. The same, perhaps, goes for the emphasis on establishing the basic techniques correctly and working on them slowly and deliberately. Putting these principles into practice, however, demands a lot more than just grasping them in theory, so you will need to keep coming back to them again and again when you practise.

4. Identifying difficulties
Each exercise or solo will present you with points of special difficulty. Once you have identified them clearly, it is these rather than the easier parts which require the greater part of your time. There is a temptation to rush through them and just hope that they will somehow become easier with time. But if you give in to the temptation, you will just be spending time practising your mistakes again and again. Analyse the difficulties carefully and give them special attention. Stick to a speed at which you can play them through correctly without any hesitation at all in the rhythm.

5. Feedback
There are several ways of getting feedback information about how your efforts are progressing.

(a) A mirror helps with checking correct posture and the positioning of right and left hands.

(b) A tape-recorder is a stern but helpful critic, especially if you can replay recordings of yourself at both normal and half speed. Wish-fulfilling day-dreams are quickly dispelled by the recorder's hypercritical ear identifying the fluffed note and missed beat one had overlooked while playing.

(c) Playing along with the cassette or a metronome, the beat of your foot, a tape-recording of *palmas* or a record will be a great help in pacing the rhythm and in identifying any irregularities in your *compás*.

153

6. Listening to Flamenco

You will find that it is very helpful to listen to as many flamenco records as you can. Later on, as part of your practice, you can try to play the *compás* along with the music or you can keep time with *palmas*. This will help you to develop a greater sense of Flamenco's crucial elements of rhythm, phrasing and *aire*.

Exercise A

The first exercise is an extension of Lesson 6 on p.19. Its main aims are to develop facility with the thumb and to increase independence and control of the left hand fingers. Each finger is kept down on the string until the ascending sequence of fingers, 1 2 3 4, has been completed on each string in turn. When you play the next adjacent string (whether higher or lower) only one finger of the left hand should move across to it at a time. The notes are played *apoyando* by the thumb. Open strings are not played this time. The pattern of left hand movements can be shown diagrammatically as follows, where each numbered dot represents a finger pressed down behind the appropriate fret. The ascending sequence at the start of the exercise is shown for notes played on the 6th string, then the 5th.

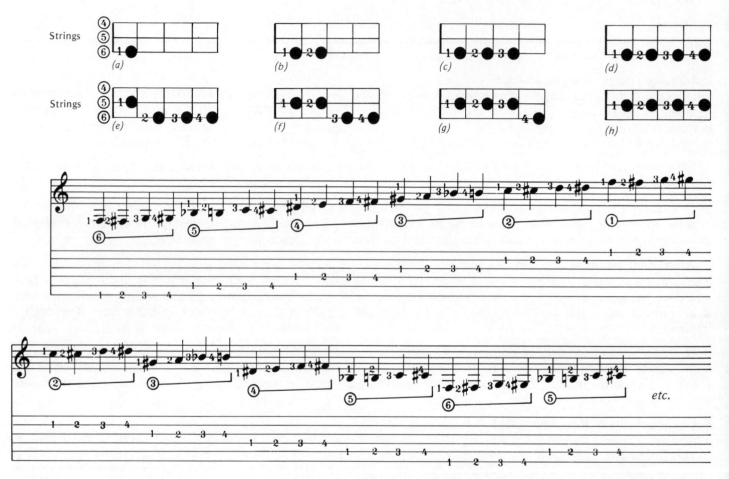

Exercises B and C

The next two exercises (B and C) are for the technique of *picado*. They provide a good means of developing your ability to play *picado* runs of single notes so that ultimately you can attain a very fast speed. Both exercises call for precise coordination of right and left hands and Exercise C will help particularly in strengthening fingers 3 and 4 of the left hand. Exercise B is played on the cassette, at the sort of speed you can ultimately aim for after you have worked up from very much slower speeds to start with.

The two exercises depend on a repeated pattern of left hand fingering, which you will learn most easily from the *cifra*. Because the pattern in each exercise is repeated the music is not written out in full, but enough is given to show how the left hand moves.

Exercise B can be varied in several ways. For example, you can start with the left hand in the 1st position and move the hand up one fret at a time instead of down as shown, or you can continue up and down the neck continuously. Alternatively, instead of moving the left hand one fret down (or up) only after all six strings have been played, you can move one fret after each group of four notes has been played on one string, moving in the same direction (up or down) after playing each string in turn. In this way the left hand will move diagonally across the fingerboard. As another alternative you can stop the notes with the left hand fingers in the order 1 2 3 4 rather than 4 3 2 1.

CASSETTE: **LESSON 26, DAILY EXERCISE B**

154

Exercise B

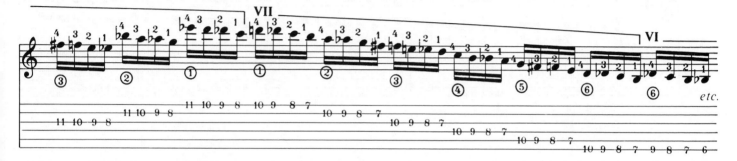

Exercise C

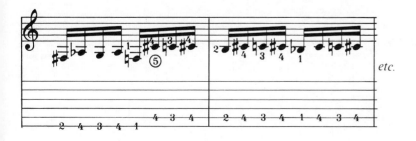

etc.

Exercise D

The following exercise is another to help you develop your *picado*. As with all the exercises, you should start very slowly, giving particular attention to the rhythm, which must be regular and even. You can increase the speed progressively. The triplets will demand rapid alternation of the fingers.

Play the exercise with all the possible right hand fingerings for *picado*, as discussed in Lesson 4, i.e. with all the following six alternations:

i — m, i — m	i — a, i — a	m — a, m — a
m — i, m — i	a — i, a — i	a — m, a — m

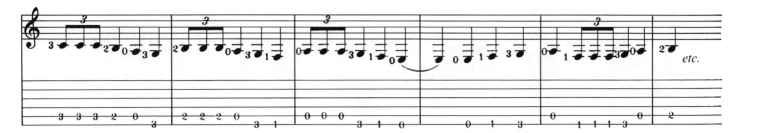

The next two exercises (E and F) take the form of extended *falsetas,* the first for Alegrías en La (A major) and the second for Soleares. The pattern of right hand fingering has already been encountered in solos. It combines *arpegios* played *tirando* (on the first two beats of the bar) with notes played *picado* (the four notes making up the third beat in each bar). Good control of the right hand is required, for there should be no movement of the hand as a whole on the changeover from *arpegio* to *picado.* The wrist stays relaxed.

The left hand movements are based on chord-positions. The fingers should take up the position of the whole chord at the beginning of each bar. The exercise will help you develop facility in changing chords rapidly with the left hand, since there should be no interruption to the flow of the melody when you change chord.

Exercise E
por Alegrías

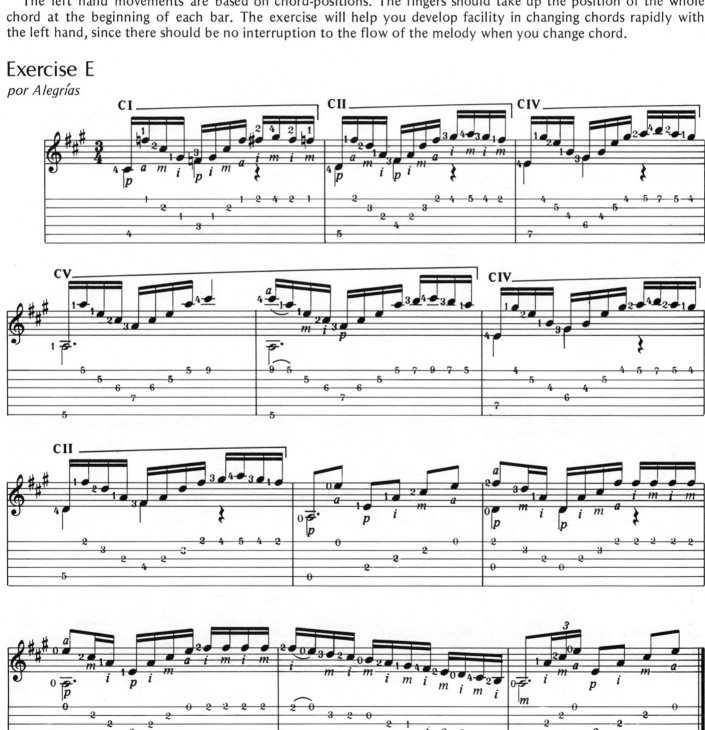

Exercise F *por Soleares*

Exercise G

Two exercises for the daily practice of *trémolo* were given in Lesson 11. Here is another *trémolo falseta*, this time for the Alegrías *en La*. The lyrical melody must flow very smoothly.

por Alegrías

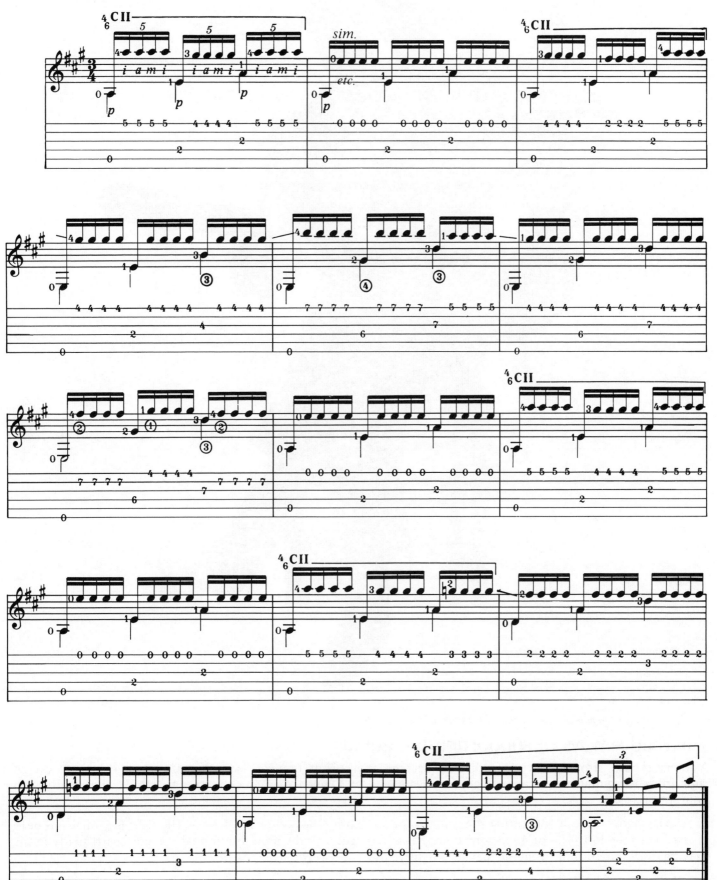

26.1 Cross-legged position for holding the guitar on the right thigh.

Alternative ways of supporting the guitar

You have been strongly advised earlier to become thoroughly familiar with the traditional flamenco way of supporting the guitar on the right thigh. Its advantages for Flamenco go much further than mere conformity with convention.

An alternative way of supporting the guitar is shown above. The hollow is rested on the right leg which has been crossed over the left. The position sometimes has advantages over the more traditional position, particularly in the playing of *picado* runs or for music making extensive use of the higher fret-positions.

Other ways of holding the guitar are sometimes advocated and may suit individual players, but their limitations tend to make them unsuitable for general recommendation.

160

Appendix A   Understanding Musical Notation

Musical notation represents music as a sequence of symbols to be read from left to right. It indicates for each individual musical sound (called a *note* in Britain and a *tone* in the U.S.A.) how high or low it is (its *pitch*) and when it occurs and how long it lasts (its *time-value*) in relation to the basic pulse or *beat* of the rhythm of the music.

Each note is represented by an oval symbol (● or ○), also called a 'note'. Notes written one above another are sounded together as a *chord*. Silences between notes (and their time-values) are represented by symbols called *rests*.

Notation can also convey other information about how the music is intended to sound and how it should be produced. We will first of all consider in more detail the representation of pitch, time-value and rhythm.

Pitch
The pitch of a musical note is determined by the speed of vibration of the source producing it, in our case the guitar string. This speed is measured as its *frequency* in cycles per second. The shorter the length of string vibrating, and hence the faster its vibration, the higher will be the frequency and the pitch of the musical note produced.

A difference in pitch between two notes is called an *interval*. When this interval is an *octave* the frequency of the higher note is exactly twice that of the lower. With each doubling of frequency the pitch rises another octave. Notes with octave intervals between them sound very similar, despite the obvious difference in pitch, because of this mathematical relationship between their frequencies.

Octaves are readily demonstrated on the guitar if, for example, we compare the note of any open string with the note obtained from the same string when it is stopped at the 12th fret. This fret lies at the midpoint of the string between nut and bridge-saddle, so that stopping the string there halves the length free to vibrate and thereby doubles the frequency of the note produced.

When the guitar is correctly tuned, the note on the 1st string stopped at the 12th fret is exactly three octaves higher than the note on the open 6th string.

Naming notes
We now need some way of naming notes of different pitch. We can name each note according to its frequency of vibration, but by convention and for greater simplicity seven letters of the alphabet, A B C D E F G, are used in recurring sequence, in order of ascending pitch from A to G.

The eighth note in a sequence upwards or downwards in pitch which is started from any of these notes will have the same letter-name as the starting note and will be an octave higher or lower, respectively. Hence the name *octave*, meaning 'eighth'.

The fact that only seven letters are used reflects the way intervals of pitch are arranged in sequence to produce a ladder of notes called a *diatonic scale*. The sequence of notes C D E F G A B C, for example, makes up one octave of the scale of C major. The interval between each adjacent pair of notes named by a letter is either a whole *tone* or, between B and C and between E and F, it is only half this amount, namely a *semitone*. On the guitar an interval of one semitone corresponds to one fret-space: i.e. moving a finger stopping the string up or down one fret alters the pitch by one semitone.

The complete ladder of pitch, in which the interval between adjacent steps is always a semitone, is called the *chromatic scale*. It has 12 different notes in it (as was illustrated by the fact that stopping a guitar-string at the 12th fret raises its pitch an octave above the note of the open string). The 5 'extra' steps in the chromatic, as opposed to a diatonic, scale will be named when we introduce the terms 'sharp' and 'flat'.

On the piano keyboard, the alphabetically named notes correspond to the white keys as follows:

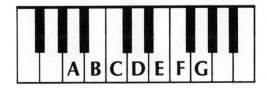

The black keys, which play sharps and flats, indicate the positions in the complete chromatic scale where the 5 'extra' steps occur. There is a semitone difference between their notes and the notes of the white keys on either side of them.

(In some Oriental music, intervals smaller than semitones may be used. Quarter-tones, for instance, commonly occur in the flamenco *Cante*. Pulling on the string from side to side with a left hand finger in the flamenco technique of *vibrato* can produce similar or smaller variations of pitch).

The notation of pitch

The pitch of a note is shown in notation by the position of its symbol on or between the five parallel lines of the

staff or *stave:*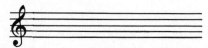

The higher up the stave the symbol is placed, the higher the pitch of the note.

The steps represented by the lines of the stave reflect the alphabetical system of naming notes. Half the distance between adjacent lines of the stave corresponds to one step along the alphabetical sequence.
Thus notes on or between lines of the stave are notated:

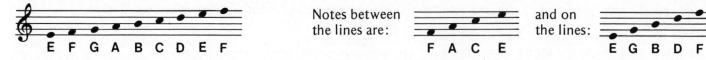

E F G A B C D E F   Notes between the lines are:  F A C E   and on the lines:  E G B D F

The symbol 𝄞 at the left-hand end of the stave is called the *treble clef.* It tells us what range of pitch is represented by 𝄞 this particular stave. The symbol derives from the letter G; it encircles the line of the stave (the second from bottom) on which the note G is represented. This G is called the *G above middle C* to indicate in which octave it occurs.

Other kinds of clef, such as the *bass clef,* which is indicated by the sign 𝄢 (and is used, for instance, to represent most of the music for the piano played by the left hand) are not found in guitar music.

We can now show how the alphabetically named notes are represented on the stave within the range of the guitar up to the 12th fret on the first string as follows:

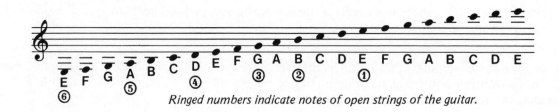

Ringed numbers indicate notes of open strings of the guitar.

As shown above, notes that are too high or too low to fit within the scope of the lines of the stave need extra lines to be drawn in for each note. These, called *leger-lines,* extend the range of the stave. The range of pitch may be extended upwards or downwards by drawing more leger-lines as required. For instance, the sixth string of the guitar may be tuned down to D for some pieces. This note is represented in notation as follows:

By convention, in order to allow the use of the treble clef and to avoid using too many leger-lines, music for the guitar is written an octave higher than it actually sounds. Thus in guitar music the G indicated by the treble clef sign actually sounds the same as the G *below* middle C on the piano.

Sharps and flats
Adding the word 'sharp' to the alphabetical name of a note indicates a note a semitone higher in pitch than the unmodified or 'natural' note. Similarly, 'flat' indicates a note one semitone lower. The symbol for sharp is ♯, for flat is ♭ and for natural, ♮ .

Thus, for example, C sharp (C♯) is a semitone higher than C:

and B flat (B♭) is a semitone lower than B:

In a scale of 'equal temperament', so called because all the semitone intervals are the same, the same note may be differently named. Thus C♯ is the same as D♭. B♯ is the same as C (since the interval from B to C is only one semitone). The 5 'extra' steps in the chromatic scale may now be named as A♯(=B♭), C♯(=D♭), D♯(=E♭), F♯(=G♭), and G♯(=A♭).

(The symbols 𝄪 and ♭♭ indicate *double sharp* and *double flat,* respectively and mean that the pitch of the note is to be raised or lowered a whole tone.)

162

Systematic rules govern the way symbols for sharp (♯), flat (♭) and natural (♮) are used in notation:

Placed at the left-hand end of each stave, they indicate that all notes in any octave, which are named the same as notes falling on the line or space they occupy, are to be played sharp or flat according to the sign used.

For example 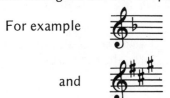 means that all B's in any octave are to be played as B flat.

and means that all F's, C's and G's in any octave are to be played sharp.

The particular pattern of sharps or flats, which are placed in a standard order on the stave, determines the *key signature* of the music and reflects the particular scale on which it is based. (The natural sign may occasionally be placed within the key signature to draw attention to a change of key.)

Placed immediately to the left of a note in the body of the notation, they are called *accidentals.* They apply to that note and to any other succeeding ones of the same pitch occurring up to but not beyond the next bar-line (a vertical line through the stave). They do not apply to similarly named notes in other octaves, which require their own symbol if they are to be modified in the same way.

The key signature may be over-ridden by a ♯, ♭, or ♮ placed to the left of any note in the notation. This is effective only in the same way already described for other accidentals. The key signature becomes operative again at the start of the next bar and may be re-emphasised by the appropriate symbol to avoid risk of confusion. An example illustrates the use of the symbols ♯ and ♭ :

C in Bar 1 is sharpened by an accidental.

B's occur in two octaves in Bars, 2, 3 and 4. The key signature dictates that all are played flat. The first two A's and the first two E's in Bar 2 are played natural; the second two of each are flat. In Bar 3, the key signature reasserts itself and A, C and E are natural.

C (this time in a higher octave) is again sharpened.

Notes available on the guitar fingerboard are shown in notation and named below. The 6 parallel lines beneath the stave represent in *cifra* the six strings of the guitar. The numbers on them show the alternative fret-positions on different strings at which the corresponding note may be sounded:

Time - values and rhythm

All music has some pattern in the way its sequence of sounds occurs over time. This pattern, or *rhythm* as it is called, may be free and without a regularly repeated structure or it may have a regular and recurring pattern of *beats* which are accented in such a way as to give the music a definite pulse.

Notes are said to have different *time-values* according to their duration relative to that of the basic beat of the rhythm. The symbols for these different time-values, as well as for their equivalent *rests*, are shown below. The names in brackets are those commonly used in the U.S.A.

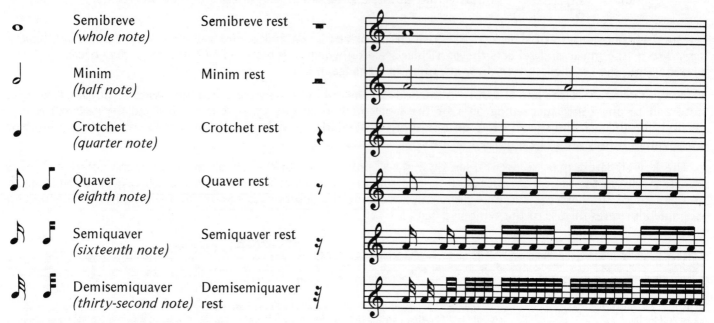

Each symbol represents a duration twice as long as the symbol next below it. Thus one semibreve is equal to 2 minims or 4 crotchets, 8 quavers, 16 semiquavers or 32 demisemiquavers.

A dot placed immediately after a note or rest prolongs the duration of that note or rest by half as much again.

Thus, 𝅗𝅥. is equal to 𝅗𝅥 plus 𝅘𝅥 and, similarly, 𝅘𝅥. equals 𝅘𝅥 plus 𝅘𝅥𝅮

A second dot increases the duration by a further half of a half, i.e. a quarter.

Thus, for example, 𝅘𝅥.. = 𝅘𝅥 plus 𝅘𝅥𝅮 plus 𝅘𝅥𝅯

When two notes of the same pitch are joined by a *tie* (e.g.: 𝅘𝅥 ⌣ 𝅗𝅥), only the first of the two notes is sounded but it is sustained for the combined duration of both the symbols.

The sign ⌢ indicates a *pause*. Placed above or below a note or rest it indicates that the note or rest is to be prolonged beyond its written time-value.

The actual, as opposed to relative, duration of each note will be determined by the speed of the music, called its *tempo*. The speed may be described (e.g. 'fast' or 'slow' or by the conventional Italian terms such as 'Presto', 'Andante' etc) or it may be indicated precisely by a metronome number showing the number of beats per minute (e.g. 𝅘𝅥 = 160). In this book the speed is indicated primarily by the recorded music on the cassette.

The *time signature* consists of two numbers written one above the other at the left-hand end of the stave at the beginning of the music or at any point in it where the rhythm changes. The lower number indicates the time-value of the unit or beat of the rhythm. Thus 4 would mean that the unit is a crotchet (quarter note) and 8, a quaver (eighth note). The upper number indicates the number of such beats in a *bar*. The duration of each bar, which is the recurring 'measure' of the rhythm, is shown as the space between vertical *bar-lines* across the stave. All bars are of equal duration if the music is played at an even speed.

Time signatures used in this book are 3/4, 4/4, 2/4, 6/8, 12/8 and, in Seguiriyas, alternating bars of 3/4 and 6/8. The first three are examples of *simple time*, demonstrated by counting aloud evenly as follows:

The symbol C is sometimes used in place of 4/4.

164

The strongest beat, and therefore the main pulse of the rhythm, is normally the first beat of the bar, but this rule very often does not apply in the written notation of Flamenco.

6/8 is an example of *compound time*, so called because the bar is divided into two beats (each equivalent to a dotted crotchet 𝅘𝅥𝅭) which are further divided into three quavers. The counting is shown as follows (*below left*):

A bar of quavers in 3/4, although of the same relative duration, has a different pulse (*above right*). The two different rhythms of 3/4 and 6/8 alternate in the flamenco *toque*, Seguiriyas.

The compound time of 12/8 is discussed in the introduction to Tientos in Lesson 17.

Time-values of beats may be combined or subdivided in any way which maintains constant the overall duration of the bar. The notes are grouped together in their notation in ways which preserve as far as possible the organisation of beats in a bar. Thus all the following bars conform to 3/4:

A *triplet* is shown in the second last bar by the figure 3 above the three notes grouped together. This indicates that three notes are played within the duration normally occupied by two of the time-value shown. Other subdivisions such as *quintuplets*, *sextuplets*, and *septuplets*, in which 5, 6 and 7 notes, respectively, occupy the duration of time normally taken by four of the same time-value are described in the text.

In the notation of Flamenco, the simple time signatures used do not adequately represent the more complex patterns of accents which occur in the various types of *compás* described in the text. Accent symbols (>) may, therefore, be needed to indicate which notes are emphasised. Time signatures, time-values and bars do, however, correctly indicate the duration and grouping of the notes relative to the basic beat of the rhythm.

Music in which the pattern of accentuation differs from the normal is said to be *syncopated*. In one sense flamenco music may be said to be syncopated to the extent that the basic *compás* displaces accents from their normal positions relative to the bar (but it must be remembered that the imposition of a conventional bar-structure on flamenco music is entirely alien to the essentially aural tradition of Flamenco). A further element of syncopation may be added when the accents are displaced from their normal positions within the *compás*. This is called *contratiempo*.

Double bar-lines indicate the end of the music or of a particular sequence of it. In the latter role they may not coincide with the end of a bar. ‖: :‖

Repeats: Passages of music enclosed within *repeat signs* (above), represented by double bar-lines with two dots facing inwards towards the music to be repeated, are played twice.
When the ending of the repeated section is played differently on the two occasions, this is indicated by the signs shown on the right:
The second time through, the music under the bracket numbered 1 is omitted and it carries on from 2.

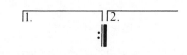

The stems of notes are by convention directed upwards (𝅘𝅥) when the note lies above the middle of the stave and downwards (𝅗𝅥) when it lies below the middle. In Flamenco, however, the sequence of the melody may be emphasised by writing all the stems upwards. Where the music has two 'voices' with, for instance, a melody on the treble strings and an accompaniment on the bass strings, each voice may be represented with its own time-values for notes and rests. Where the melody and bass notes coincide, as in the initial bass E of the following ending-phrase from Soleares, both time-values may be shown simultaneously:

The upward stems and grouping of the tails of the first four notes indicate that the triplet (occupying half a beat) starts one quaver's duration after the initial E. The lower voice shows the E as a dotted minim, the only note in the bass voice in the bar. This indicates that the sound is allowed to sustain throughout the bar. In guitar music it is often difficult to show simply how long each note is sustained.

In Flamenco, only parts of the music are clearly audible as consisting of two voices. If one or the other voice is absent throughout a whole bar rests are not written for that bar. Throughout the music in the book complicated ways of representing voicing in the music have been largely avoided since the cassette will help you hear clearly how the notes should sound. You will also find it helpful to try to think in terms of left hand chord positions, which in Flamenco are very often held down by the left hand fingers while a melody is built up around the chord.

More symbols: grace-notes and ornaments

In some of the pieces of music in this book you will see occasional notes or groups of notes written much smaller than the others. These are *grace-notes* which here indicate an embellishment played very rapidly. You will be able to hear the correct timing from the cassette. They must not hold up the *compás* and as a general rule in this book they are played *before* the main beat of the rhythm.

An example of the use of grace-notes is found in the introduction to the Soleá in Lesson 22 (*top right*).

There is only one other *ornament* indicated by a special symbol in this book and this is the *upper mordent*. The symbol ᵚ above a note means that the note is to be alternated once very rapidly with the note next above it in the scale by means of 'hammering on' and 'pulling off'.

An example of the mordent (*right*) is seen in Lesson 24.

Scales

The starting note of a diatonic scale is called the *tonic* or keynote. The 8 ascending steps of the scale are numbered from it as *degrees* of the scale as far as the 8th degree which is the octave of the starting note. The number of semitones in the intervals between the tonic and each degree defines the character of the scale.

In a *major* scale, the intervals between degrees of the scale are shown as follows, taking the scale of C major as an example:

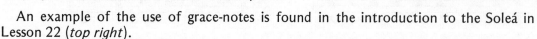

Music based on this scale is said to be in the *key* of C major. The key signature has no sharps or flats:

Flamenco players traditionally name keys according to the tonic sol-fa system, which names the notes of the C major scale as:

C	D	E	F	G	A	B	C
do	re	mi	fa	so	la	ti	do

Any key which uses the left hand fingering and chord shapes pertaining to C major when the guitar is played without a *cejilla* is called 'do' by flamencos, even when the *cejilla* alters the pitch from an actual C.

Any of the 12 different notes in the chromatic scale may be taken as a keynote, the intervals between the degrees remaining constant for all major scales. Thus a scale of A major contains the notes:

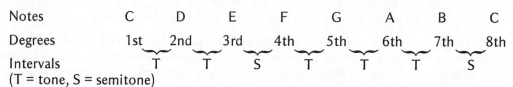

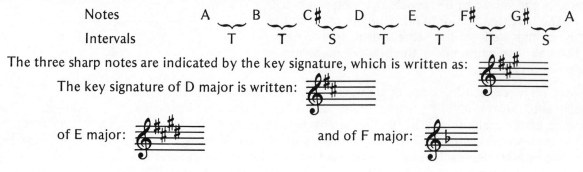

Not only the first degree (the *tonic*) but all the other degrees of a scale also have special names. Those of particular importance in the chords most commonly used are the 4th degree (the *subdominant*), the 5th (the *dominant*) and the 7th (the *leading note*).

166

Minor scales

Minor scales are characterised by having only a semitone interval between 2nd and 3rd degrees.

In a *harmonic minor* scale (which is more of theoretical than practical importance) the scale is constructed as follows, with three semitones between 6th and 7th degrees:

Degrees	1		2		3		4		5		6		7		8
Intervals		T		S		T		T		S		T+S		S	

In the *melodic minor* scale there are two alternative endings to the scale, the choice depending on whether the scale is ascending or descending, as follows:

ASCENDING

Degrees	1		2		3		4		5		6		7		8
Intervals		T		S		T		T		T		T		S	

DESCENDING

Degrees	8		7		6		5		4		3		2		1
Intervals		T		T		S		T		T		S		T	

These minor scales may be illustrated for A minor, one of the minor scales most often used in Flamenco:

A B C D E F G♯ A	A B C D E F♯ G♯ A	A G F E D C B A
Harmonic Minor	Ascending Melodic	Descending Melodic Minor

The key signature for A minor is the same as for C major, so that the key is said to be the *relative minor* of C major. The minor scale with the same tonic as the major scale is called the *tonic minor*. For C it is C minor, whose key signature has three flats:

Other minor keys commonly used in Flamenco are D minor (the relative minor of F major), and E minor (the relative minor of G major).

D minor

E minor

Appendix B   Flamenco Scales and the Phrygian Mode

There is a special kind of scale in Flamenco which is of even more fundamental importance than either major or minor scales, since it is the basis for the music of Soleares, Seguiriyas, Fandangos, Tangos, Bulerías and related *toques*. This has close similarities to the scale known to classical musicians as the Phrygian mode.

Modal scales were originally based on sequences of the natural notes A B C D E F G. Their Greek names reflect their use in early ecclesiastical music (the scale of C major was formerly called the Ionian mode) and the term 'mode' refers to the different characters of the scales produced by starting from different notes of the natural scale. The Phrygian mode is based on the scale E F G A B C D E. Its particular character depends on the fact that there is a semitone between its 1st and 2nd degrees and between its 5th and 6th degrees.

Scales in the form of the Phrygian mode can be constructed from other starting notes than E if the sequence of intervals (S T T T S T T) is preserved. The Phrygian mode starting on E is written with the same key signature as C major or its relative minor, A minor, i.e. without sharps or flats. In Flamenco, we also find similar modal scales started on A (played in the position called *por medio* on the guitar) and written with the same key signature as

F major or D minor (i.e.   ) or on F♯ (key signature of D major or B minor   ) or on B (key

signature G major or E minor   ).

Again, as mentioned before, the flamenco name of the scale is determined by the positions for fingering it on the guitar rather than by its actual pitch, which depends on the fret-position of the *cejilla*.

We may call the characteristic flamenco scale the Phrygian mode for convenience, but it is not quite the same as the Phrygian mode known to classical musicians. In Flamenco the scale may include the leading note of the relative minor written in the same key signature. This note (e.g. G♯ in the scale based on E) is used in the harmonies of the music, which keep returning to the major chord of the starting note. Also, when G♯ is substituted for G in melodic passages based on the scale from E (i.e. when the 3rd degree is sharpened) the music has a characteristically oriental quality. This is especially pronounced when melodic phrases are based on the *pentatonic* scale of 5 notes (e.g. E F G♯ A B). Accidentals are required in the notation to indicate when this note is sharpened or when its equivalent in other keys is played (e.g. C♯ in *por medio*).

Throughout this book the modal type of scale used in many flamenco *toques* is referred to as the Phrygian mode, although it must be said that the historical reasons for its role in Flamenco are still obscure. The adoption by the early Church in Spain of Byzantine music may be, as de Falla argued in his writings on *Cante Jondo*, the decisive historical event. Early ecclesiastical influences on the development of folk-music may well have been important but the unique characteristics of the scales used in Flamenco suggest that other influences, some *gitano*, some Islamic, are also likely to have contributed to the evolution of the typical structure of flamenco scales and harmonies. The subject is clearly a large and complex one, beyond the scope of this volume.

Chords and harmony

Some simple principles about the use of chords and harmony in flamenco music will now be briefly outlined.

Naming intervals
As we have seen from the name *octave*, intervals are named numerically according to the total number of letters encompassed. Thus A to C (three letters) is a *third*, A to E (five letters) is a *fifth* and A to G (seven letters) is a *seventh*. The numbering is not affected by sharps or flats, depending only on the letter-names of the notes in question. The numerical name is, however, qualified according to the number of semitones in the interval. Thus there are 4 semitones in a *major third* (e.g. C to E), 3 in a *minor third* (e.g. A to C), 7 in a *perfect fifth* (e.g. C to G), 10 in a *minor seventh* (e.g. G to F), 11 in a *major seventh* (e.g. C to B). *Augmented* and *diminished* are other qualifying terms used in specific contexts.

Building simple chords
The simplest three-note chords are called *triads*. *Major triads* are built up from a starting note (the *root*) together with a major third and a major fifth. Thus the chord of C major contains the notes C E and G. *Minor triads* are similar except that the third is minor, not major. Thus the chord A minor contains A C and E. Notes of the chord may be doubled or tripled in different octaves. They may also be arranged in alternative orders of pitch to give different *inversions* of the chord. The most solid and restful sounding of these will be the one where the root is the lowest note.

Chord sequences
In any major key, whether in Flamenco or elsewhere, the major chord of the tonic is the most important, together with those of the subdominant and the dominant. A fourth note is added to the dominant to make a *dominant seventh*, so called because the extra note is a minor seventh above the dominant.

In the key of C major, for example, the main chords are C major (the tonic), F major (subdominant) and G7 (as the dominant seventh is written). The dominant seventh has a feeling of tension in it, resolved by a return to the tonic. In the key of A minor, the corresponding chords are A minor, D minor and E7. A minor seventh is commonly added to the tonic in the progression to the subdominant major chord, as in the sequence C C7 F.

In flamenco music based on the Phrygian type of modal scale the chord to which the music tends repeatedly to return at the end of passages of melody or rhythm is the major chord of the starting note of the scale. There is a very characteristic descending sequence or *cadence* which provides a basis for both melodic and rhythmic passages. In the Phrygian mode based on E the cadence is A minor, G major, F major, E major. The minor chord at the beginning may be replaced by the major chord to which it is the relative minor and this and the other three chords may, in some sequences, have the addition of minor sevenths to give, for example, the sequence C (or C7), G7, F7, E7. Other variants on this basic pattern are common. In the *por medio* key, corresponding chords are D minor (or F major), C major (or C7), B♭ (or sometimes B♭7) and A (or sometimes A7). In Bulerías, for example, you will find that some *compases* end on A7 rather than A.

Other passages of the music in the same piece or *toque* may use alternative progressions derived from the three main chords of the major key or its relative minor key with the same key signature (e.g. G7, C and F in music based on the Phrygian mode starting on E). Such progressions are very common in the accompaniment of the *Cante* or in solo guitar passages based on it.

In recent years more complex *chromatic* harmonies and jazz-influenced chord substitutions, augmented and diminished chords and chords with added major 7th, 6th or 9th have been introduced into Flamenco. Some embellished chords of this type belong to the earliest traditions of Flamenco. A discussion of their use is beyond the scope of the present volume, but any such chords in the music included here are mentioned in the text (e.g. the chord of F major 7 with FACE played in the First Soleares).

168